The Heart On

"A profound and experiential book about the love of being human. She details what it takes to open the heart and heal from within. An empowering journey that liberates you to look deeply into the mind, body, and spirit. This enlightening book invites you to escape and explore the levels of your heart while riding the waves of grief and sorrow helping you to navigate your emotional ups and downs.

Asttarte's story is personal, experiential, and authentic coming from a true Shaman she understands that it takes two people to grow and bask in the source of love. I highly recommend this book for couples."

Anita DeFrancesco, MA
Author of *Live Free: Re-Create & Liberate Your Life* and *The Donna Gentile Story*. Founder of Tantra Wisdom, Discover Joyous Love Podcast, www.TantraWisdom.com

"Asttarte and Paavo bravely share the depth and struggles of their intimate sexual relationship in a way that captures not only their commitment and love, but also serves as a model for couples who want to work through their traumas together to emerge whole and connected."

Fredric E. Rabinowitz, Ph.D. Psychologist and Author of the books: *Man Alive, Deepening Psychotherapy with Men, Men and Depression, Breaking Barriers in Counseling Men*, and *Deepening Group Psychotherapy with Men*.

"Asttarte pours out her personal experiences of healing with courage and devotion, empowering and encouraging others to follow her example. Through her stories, she reveals what it takes to bring untamed sexual energy fully into the heart."

Amrita Grace, Author of *"Reclaiming Aphrodite-The Journey to Sexual Wholeness"*

"In *The Heart On; Opening The Heart of Your Beloved,* Asttarte guides us in how we can be ourselves, stand in our power and live a life of love, the life we truly desire. For anyone seeking to awaken to their true nature and what's possible in creating their reality, I highly recommend this book."

-Laurie Handlers, author of *Sex & Happiness: The Tantric Laws of Intimacy*, Speaker/Facilitator/Coach

"This beautiful book begins with an etheric/earthy poem written by Paavo, who is the Beloved of the author and is now on the other side of the veil. As Paavo and Asttarte weave a colorful story-telling cloth throughout the pages, they allow themselves to be vulnerable. Self-identifying as "a polyamorous Dakini, and free loving spirit," she positions herself to be both teacher and student, healer and one being healed in the course of her relationship with Paavo. The book is their story, sometimes messy, sometimes sublime, but also that of so many other perfectly imperfect individuals who are in partnership. Each person comes into a relationship toting baggage from childhood and previous partnerships. She delves into the impact of trauma and ways to address it in the presence of one you wish to trust in holding your heart sacred. The author expressed that the Beloved in one's life is a reflection of the Divine and the interactions can be transcendent."

- Edie Weinstein, MSW, LSW, Creator of *By Divine Design*, Best Selling Author of *The Bliss Mistress Guide to Transforming The Ordinary into the Extraordinary*, Edie offered her first TedX talk called Overcoming the Taboo of Touch. She is a Certified Cuddle Party Facilitator.

The Heart On   Asttarte Deva

THE HEART ON

The Heart On   Asttarte Deva

THE HEART ON

Opening The Heart of Your Beloved

Through Tantra, The Breath, The Art of Listening, Submission & Dominance in Intimate Relationships

By Asttarte Deva
Foreword by: Jan Cocke

A Guide for Couples & Tantra Healers

Author of Awaken to Living, Tantra for Your Whole Life

The Heart On; Opening The Heart of Your Beloved,
Through Tantra, The Breath, The Art of Listening, Submission & Dominance in Intimate Relationships, A Guide for Couples & Tantra Healers, by Asttarte Deva

Copyright 2023 by Asttarte Deva
ISBN Print Version: 979-8-218-19260-0
ISBN Hardcover Version: 9798391351269

Genre: Tantra/Relationships/Sacred Sexuality

First Edition, 2023

All Rights Reserved.
Printed in the United States
No part of this book may be reproduced or used in any manner without the written permission of the author except in cases of brief quotations cited in articles or reviews.

Cover Photo, Copywrite by Asttarte Deva

Published by: Asttarte Deva Publishing

Names have been changed to protect their privacy.

Dedicated to my Beloved Paul Cook. For without you, this work would not have been created. I love you forever.

To my Dear Beloved Paul

I want to thank you for your commitment, dedication, devotion, love, and service to me as your Beloved. All you wanted to do was make me laugh and help me heal, and you did just that.

You wanted to become a Healer, and you ended in this life by becoming a Master Healer. You became my personal Healer. With all my 20 years of training in different Healing Modalities, I never experienced the deep profound Healing I needed to receive. It was only until after I met you, and trained you in all, or many of my modalities and teachings that I finally received the true healing that I needed to work through my deep core self. You didn't stay with us to see the result of my transformation, but I know you are watching from the other side.

The Spirit Medicine work was the end practice that helped bring this all to fruition and bring it full circle. I am now transformed. I have you to thank for this.

You were and are a true Master Paul and I am forever grateful for you becoming my Teacher and Healer and stepping into my life to be a stand for me. You got to experience the benefits of what it is like to be a Healer for someone else. And I got to be a stand for you to fully step into your power and become the Leader and Healer you were always meant to be. I love you, Paul. Love, Asttarte

The Heart On   Asttarte Deva

Sun Rises, by Paavo

Sun Rises, eyes meeting
Gazing between the shadow of the light
Nighttime brought dreams
Angel, singing with joy
Celebration
Marching through the Clouds
Wind Chimes Screaming
Soul searching
Finding presence
Our bodies marching as the birds are chirping
Trusting, caressing – staring into her eyes
As I reach across the meadows
Our worlds unite
Finger tips tingle
Longing – river appears – wetness
Slow, slower, slower
Ask for entrance
Wish has been granted.

The Heart On   Asttarte Deva

Contents

Feelings Buried Alive Never Die / 17
Dedication, by Paavo / 19
Forward, by Jan Cocke / 21
Preface by Asttarte Deva / 27
Introduction, The Why and History of The Heart On / 31

Section 1: Your Man's Orders and Training Him to Heal You / 35
My Story of the Beginning of My Man Becoming a Healer for Me / 37
Training Your Man to Heal You / 41
After My Beloved Received his Kundalini Reiki Master Attunement – a story / 44
Making Requests / 47
Teach Him to Be a Gentleman or Fire Him / 49
Being a Shiva for the Goddess / 51
How BDSM Saved My Marriage / 52
Learning A New Sexual Experience / 55
Wild Tantric Review / 59

King of Hearts, a poem by Mother Teresa / 63

Section 2: Healing Her; Being a Shiva for the Goddess / 65
When I Gaze Into Her Eyes / 67
Holding the Space for Your Wife or Girlfriend / 69
A Man That Loves You / 70
Healing Your Woman / 75
Surrendering to Your Man - A Guide for Women / 77

Your Man as Your Healer / 79
Women's Emotional Trauma / 81
Hugging a Woman for Healing / 82
Follow the Leader Breath / 84
It Takes Two / 86
Daka's Orders / 88
Exercise: Tantra Yoni Chakra Work / 89
Exercise: How to Help Your Woman *and Dissolve her Armor and Ice* / 93
Wild Tantric Review / 97

Section 3: The Love Cock / 103
The Love Cock / 105
The Angry Cock / 107
Why is it the men are Always Sexually Frustrated? / 110
When You Get Involved out of Sex / 112
Exercise: How to Use your Love Cock Instead of Your Angry Cock / 113
Maintaining the Love Cock through Semen Retention / 114
The Love Cock as a Path of Intimacy & Enlightenment / 117
When the Love Cock Triggers the Woman / 121

Section 4: An Intimate Exploration to Healing Her Trauma with the Love Cock / 125
Exercise Day 1 / 127
Exercise Day 2 / 129
Exercise Day 3 / 131
Exercise Day 4 / 133
Exercise Day 5 / 134

Section 5: She Healing Him / 137
Shakti's Orders / 139

Helping the Woman by Healing the Man / 141
The Forbidden Fruit / 143
Hugging a Man for Healing & The Love Cock / 146
Belly Massage / 148
Enchanted Heart, a poem, by Paavo / 151

Section 6: For Couples / 155
Understanding Intimacy / 157
Understanding Tantric Energy Between Two Lovers / 159
Letting My Beloved into My Heart / 165
Holding Space for Him / 167
Listen More Speak Less / 171
Relationships as a Tool for Growth / 173
Writing Exercise: Questions for Couples / 176
Wild Tantric Review / 179

Section 7: Tantric & Relationship Exercises for Keeping the Heart Open / 183
Some Tantra Practices You Can Start With / 185
Kundalini Orgasmic Meditation / 188
Intimacy and Touch / 190
Relationship Vision / 191
Gratitude Checklist / 193
Start the Day Ritual / 194
Phrases to Hang on the Walls / 196

Appendix: The Brain is the Block to Your…/ 201
Recommended Books / 202
Dedications / 205
About the Author / 209

The Heart On   Asttarte Deva

"What you may not realize is that when negative feelings are not resolved as they occur, these feelings remain very much alive in your physical energy field (body) and these feelings affect each day of your life."

--Feelings Buried Alive Never Die, by: Karol K Truman

The Heart On   Asttarte Deva

To My Beloved Asttarte, you are my soul mate, Lover, Beloved, my everything. My life will be complete because we met. Never did I expect to find you in this lifetime. You are my everything. We will be tied to everlasting eternity.

Love you, Paavo

The Heart On   Asttarte Deva

Forward

The Heart On is a rare glimpse into the heart-opening, healing power of conscious relationships. Featuring a variety of healing modalities including Tantra and even Reiki, discover how you, too, can build trust and safety while opening your heart in the arms of your Beloved.

This heart-warming and life-enhancing book is beautifully written, a wonder-filled gift to the world and wonderful tribute to Paavo.

It is, as the author writes, a "profound journey of intention of coming to the heart" in which "your whole being will radiate bliss, love, and light." Wow!

Nevertheless, conscious relationships have the uncanny capacity to bring up unresolved and unconscious issues, patterns, and beliefs. *The Heart On* is an inspiring "journey of two wounded healers, coming together to help each other grow to the next level of their evolution."

The author and her Beloved are vulnerable, real, honest, and direct. On the pages of this book, you will find descriptions of many unresolved issues, patterns and beliefs that came up for one or both as well as tools they used to transform them.

There's no boasting or taking a holier-than-thou stance, which is refreshing especially in the Tantra field. The Beloveds treat each other with respect. They listen and feel heard. Theirs is a dance of ebb and flow, leading and following, giving, and receiving.

Both Beloveds describe in exquisite detail the value of leading from the heart, not just their sexual energies. "After being fully present, being real, authentic, able to truly understand another's world of what they are dealing with and what really matters to another, learning how to not react and calm the brain that always tries to run the show and practicing many tools for healing on each other, processing the emotions that were blocked inside our bodies, our hearts and our soul, we have created the most magical, loving, fun, and powerful relationship we've ever had in our entire lives."

You'll read captivating stories as Asttarte and Paavo travel down the road less traveled. As a sneak peek, here are just a few jewels that grabbed my attention and a tiny bit of commentary:

Section 1: Your Man's Orders and Training

A polyamorous Dakini for 20 years, Asttarte "prayed out to the universe with a powerful intention that it was my turn to have the love that I helped everyone else so much to open to, and return to me." That's a compelling and dynamic statement to the universe! "It was always about them, the other, giving, but no receiving, and no opening."

Brutally honest with herself, she adds, "there was no balance, and all that was left was a waiting, a longing for something bigger, greater, and more profound than I had ever experienced before."

As a result, the door to her heart opened, and her true self and her man walked in.

Their training included initiating him to Reiki. Reiki? Hmmm... What a great idea!

"Combining Reiki with Tantra is a perfect blend of energy healing, clearing, awareness, and kundalini opening, expansion, and bliss."

She asserts that during training, if your man won't listen or respect you, "Fire him"! Great advice!

Section 2: Healing Her and Being a Shiva for the Goddess

Many healers I know talk about the importance of "holding space" without judgment for others. In Section 2, you'll find practical tips for holding space and being fully present with and for your Beloved.

You'll receive direct advice around healing the "core of your traumas and receive the love you have been longing for like I have," as well as healing your inner child. For those with experience in healing work and Yoni work, check out the description of the Tantra Yoni Chakra Work exercise and tips to release stuck emotional energy.

Asttarte's honest insights around dissolving her own armor and ICE is full of humility and love. She reminds us that healing and transformation that take place within the safe space of your relationship will produce the greatest results, magic will be created, and like in their relationship, "their hearts opened and healed and their love for their beloved skyrocketed."

Section 3: The Love Cock

For women, Asttarte gives expert advice! For example, a man's erection when viewed from a "loving relationship and coming into the sexual experience with love, his hardness is not something that needs to be utilized immediately." As an alternative, she suggests that "it actually produces more healing for him and for his woman when he can keep his hard cock, and hold her, lay with her, cuddle her, whether clothes are on or off, and be outside his woman. She can feel his commitment, his intensity, his passion for her, and yet she can feel safe knowing there is no expectation for anything to happen."

For men, she invites us to become more sensitive to how "young girls often go through life, having to defend themselves, fight off people who cross their boundaries where they feel threatened just for being soft, feminine and girly." Her sincere wish is "for all men to learn to listen, to hear what the women of their world truly need and to open your hearts to love them. This then, is when the women of the world will TRULY give you ALL the love you ever wanted!"

Section 4: An Intimate Exploration to Healing Her Trauma with the Love Cock

"Sexual problems," says relationship expert Dr. Kathlyn Hendricks, "are seldom about sex. They are almost always about a kink in the (energy) hose right here (pointing to her throat)." Asttarte describes the pain of "feeling trapped, unable to breathe or move, but knew it was trapped emotions that made me feel this way." "It felt like a harness around my neck, like a huge slave collar around my neck..."

On the "third day in a row of working on opening my Throat Chakra," her Beloved Paavo invited her to use her words and "tell me how you feel." "Sad, confused, scared, disappointed, angry, misunderstood, unloved, stupid." After opening her throat, she adds that Paavo was "overjoyed with amazement, as he felt my connection… like the beginning honeymoon phase of our relationship nearly two years prior."

Section 5: She Healing Him

Section 5 starts with a reminder that we need balance in our relationships. It describes the inequality that can emerge after receiving. When you switch roles while you are still healing from past traumas, "you can feel in your power again by affirming your boundaries, making requests of him to ask you before he touches you and this brings up vulnerability in him."

"However, as women, especially with past traumas, we need to be asked before anything to feel ok, to feel safe, and to feel in our power." "In coming to balance I see the perspective from both angles. Women often fear being vulnerable with the men, and men often become angry and frustrated that their women are unresponsive."

"The real truth is it's all about timing. If one partner has needs that are not being fulfilled because they expect them to be met on their timing, but his partner needs to go at a different pace, they may in fact interpret it as though they are not being loved, rejected or worst-case scenario, abandoned."

"But the truth is one partner needs to open slower, gentler, and with more presence, calmness, and tenderness. Miscommunications are bound to happen when the speed and pace of each other is met at different paces. It is best to try to sort out these differences early on, or it could become a problem with maintaining intimacy later." Important advice!

For men, you'll learn how "a woman's breasts are an extension of her heart chakra" and "a very sacred part of her body." "To avoid feeling rejected, pause and wait."

For women, you'll learn that "when a man allows you to massage his belly, he is giving you permission to touch his heart." "A man's vulnerability often starts with his belly, as he unravels his armor for touch, and gets closer to his needs for being loved, his heart slowly starts to melt and open."

Section 6: For Couples

I like how this section stresses the importance of mastering communication skills like improving your listening skills. In my vernacular, the three levels of resonant listening are 1) listen for accuracy (of what they're saying), 2) listen for empathy [appreciate the core feeling(s) under the speaker's experience like sadness, fear, anger, joy, sexual feelings], and 3) listen for mutual creativity.

Section 6 is about healing ourselves, gaining strength together, and living "in alignment with a strong solid committed loving relationship." "As we trust the flow of energy within ourselves, create a rhythm of love making at each appropriate and perfect time, be consistent with spiritual energy practices and support towards our goals as leaders, teachers, coaches and healers of the community, we will continue letting go of the small stuff."

I appreciate reading about "how all the chemicals in his brain had just gone haywire for a little while" during an experience of not feeling worthy. I laughed when I read about her trying on sexy lingerie from her early 20's that burst his story bubble. "He realized that his feelings of not being worthy had come up, and the anger that he had was that he didn't know how to receive love. He didn't know how to take my love in, and he just wanted to shout it out because he was afraid."

Addressing relationships as opportunities for growth, Asttarte adds, "Relationships are growth when you love someone and all the issues that have to do with love come to the surface, fear of loss, fear of abandonment, fear of rejection, fear of being controlled, fear of suffocation, air, sabotage, fear of losing one's identity, fear of losing one's individuality and independence, and all such fears that have to either do with coming closer to the soul self, or the other."

Section 7: Tantric & Relationship Exercises for Keeping the Heart Open

There are many jewels in Section 7 in the form of practical practices to keep the heart open. One that I'm particularly fond of is the list of positive affirmations or phrases that you can post around the house.

Humbly, I honor and thank Asttarte and Paavo, for this masterpiece, for doing your own inner work, and for sharing your intimate experiences and lessons learned with the world.

Thank you for *The Heart On*!

Namaste,

Jan Cocke
Best-Selling Author & Award-Winning Producer

P.s. I appreciate you dedicating the song "Honey, I'm Good" by Andy Grammer to your Beloved Paavo. I checked out the song. Wow! It's now one of my favorites!

Preface by Asttarte

In the Beginning:

I'm doing something that's a first for me, something I've never done. This man is growing to be someone I care about and I'm really letting my heart open to him. I'm being vulnerable. I'm being real. I'm being powerful and dominant. I'm being honest and direct. And I'm being emotional and trusting. I'm being treated with respect, and I feel understood. I feel honored and really cared for and taken care of and heard. And, the amazing thing is, he has my son's dad's birthday.

He's helping me understand my son's father and love him, grieve him, and know how he feels deeper in his heart because this beautiful being is in his heart with me, and felt a lot of the same things my sons father felt but never processed them. He's honest about where he's at with them. He's healed the incestual too close to Mommy Jewish stuff where mom treated him like a surrogate partner. He's healed where he wasn't allowed to put his wife first, and mom was competitive and wanted to treat her as #1 (runs in many Jewish families). His mom was competitive with her and never accepted his wife because she wanted his attention and he healed that. He healed feeling like a bully as a kid, being made fun of and all the misdirected sexual energy. He healed feeling inadequate and not good enough and where he felt small.

He healed feeling like he always had to Dominate and could never allow himself to be submissive and never even knew he was dominant before. He learned where he took over conversations and didn't let others speak or let them feel or express themselves.

He learned where his heart was guarded. He's finally letting himself be vulnerable where he shut himself off before. My previous love still had to dominate conversations and never listened to me, never surrendered to me or let me lead. He was too scared, angry, and afraid to let go of control. The ability to communicate all of this has been so powerful for me, the revelations, the understanding.

He's so opening my heart. And I'm so opening his. We both never experienced leading from the heart before and not having sex. Just feeling the love and the energy. And he's really listening to me, and he really trusts me. These are all things I wanted with my ex. It's like he's helping me experience my ex in the eyes of someone who has worked through the issues he had and actually healed them. He cried with me for my ex that he never healed these things, and yet as a prayer and in hopes one day he finally does.

My love, Paavo, he doesn't care what we do and if I want to lead, he lets me. If I want him to lead, he'll easily switch into that role and surrenders to whichever way I want to go. He says he's a virgin when it comes to sex, sexual expression through words, domination, orgasm, and even female genital massage. He had not learned or experienced much prior to meeting me in those regards, but he surrenders to what I choose to teach, guide, or instruct in each moment.

Later on, as the Years Went By:

After a dozen Shamanic Journeys, powerful Sacred Native American Plant Medicine, completing the entire curriculum for Living with Landmark, the Team Management and Leadership Program and learning tons of distinctions in Communication, we have the life we love. After being fully present, being real, authentic, able to truly understand another's world of what they are dealing with and what really matters to another, learning how to not react and calm the brain that always tries to run the show and practicing many tools for healing on each other, processing the emotions that were blocked inside our bodies, our hearts and our soul, we have created the most magical, loving, fun and powerful relationship we've ever had in our entire lives. And, we have chosen to become Leaders to help and teach others to have the same amazing experience in their lives as well.

An amazing relationship doesn't happen all by itself. Understanding another, and being able to listen, be loving, able to give and receive and a contribution to others doesn't come naturally, especially after a lifetime of challenges, hurts, struggles, traumas, rejections, abandonment, and pains. However, when you've found someone who is just as committed to personal growth, and having deep profound love as you do, things do ultimately come to a place of feeling like a magical miracle. And, no, they didn't come all by themselves. It takes enormous commitment, determination, power, surrender, hope and the ability to ask questions and the ability to not just ask for help, but have the will to follow through -- stick with it, the knowledge and education to support the help, and the follow through to keep it going, keep on asking, and keep on surrendering over and over again.

The Heart On   Asttarte Deva

Introduction

In this book on Tantra, The Heart On, Opening The Heart of Your Beloved, Through Tantra, The Breath, The Art of Listening, Submission & Dominance in Intimate Relationships, A Guide for Couples and Tantra Healers, I talk about how my Beloved and I are teachers to each other, and how to help couples unravel the layers of energy in their auric field and their physical body to create deeper intimacy with each other. It is a manual for couples and practitioners on how to work on each other, and help their partner surrender to them, be present, and accept the love they are receiving. It is also on how to be powerful in one's approach to be dominant and in that dominance, it helps their partner to relax, and trust it is coming from a place of love, and to surrender into the arms of your Beloved (or practitioner).

The Why and the history of "The Heart On" comes from having been a Tantra practitioner for most of my adult life (around 20 years or so), and having lived from the root chakra all of those years, until finally having a kundalini awakening in a profound journey of intention of coming to the heart, and with the grand finale of going to an Ayahuasca Healing Ceremony and raising the energy from the root center and bringing it up to the heart space. The journey of opening the heart has been a lifelong journey, and when I finally found the man of my dreams during the same time as having this awakening in a private journey, the two came together at the perfect moment.

When you live out of the root chakra, the sex center, it can be very intimidating to a lot of people who are in your presence. They can feel your height of sexual energy. They can feel as though you want them all and be turned on by you and you can easily manipulate people with your sexual power, but when you are integrated from the root center and the heart center, the energy you radiate feels different. It feels softer, lighter.

The people around you may feel your pure intention. They may still feel your sexual energy, but they also will feel your heart energy and that will help them feel safe, supported, and loved. When you are with your beloved and partner in person, who you are with will feel you are coming from both your root center and your heart center. Your partner will have a less easy time to melt into your arms when you are radiating energy from the root center, the sex center. It will feel more like an addictive energy and obsession or prowess, like a hunger need of an animal. It may feel radical and wild, and sexy, but it may also not feel as safe. After the energies re-align from the heart to the root, and then from the root to heart, you and your partner will feel you integrated and come together in oneness. Your power source will come from all centers and your whole being will radiate bliss, love, and light.

The Why and the history of The Heart On is a combination of two beloveds, who had spent a combination of over 55 years of healing and recovery. In our discovery and collective healing vitality, we have created a way to help support other couples to help them heal. And work through issues that come up for them in partnership.

All couples need different things to help them work through their personal combined collective and ancestral patterns and issues that they bring together. Using your intuition, your inner power, and your inner voice, you can transform and release anything that the partnership is confronted by and dealing with. In many ways, in the old days where there were arranged marriages, and eventually couples fell in love, became close, and were happy. It makes sense that couples that struggle today can actually heal and work through whatever it is that they're dealing with.

In my view, any two people can come together and work through issues, patterns and beliefs with the right intention and commitment. Not everyone is compatible, but anyone can transform anything when they chose to.

This is a journey of two wounded healers, coming together to help each other grow to the next level of their evolution.

When two people come together and fall in love for the right reasons, miracles can happen. History is created and love unfolds. We all want to have real love, and we all want it to come from the truth of who we are rather than it being something that we make up, we force or pretend.

Sometimes fear arises on the journey of looking for love, and even on the journey after finding love. Often fear is a sabotage that separates a partnership when you can work through the fear and love your partner anyway, both can melt. Both people in a partnership can find peace and both can find bliss together.

I hope this book brings you comfort, brings you passion, brings you excitement, and brings you joy. May it help you to open your heart to your beloved and learn new tools that you can use together. May it serve you well.

After nearly the completion of this writing, my beloved, had manifested an illness and passed away July 27, 2022. The publishing of this great work is in honor of him, so his story carries on. "You will forever be remembered in history my love." *Love never dies.*

The Heart On   Asttarte Deva

Section 1: Your Man's Orders and Training Him to Heal You

The Heart On   Asttarte Deva

My Story of the Beginning of My Man Becoming a Healer for Me

As a polyamorous Dakini, and free loving spirit as I am, I discovered that the true gift of life is to connect with the Daka of my dreams; the man who loves me, feels me, sees me, hears me, and honors me, and with every breath, we feel each other and connect our souls. He helps me open my soul and truly heal. I've been waiting my whole life for this man, this man of my dreams.

It takes a willing determination to find your man, and be a stand that he honors you, and as he honors you, he listens to what you need. And as a woman discovers what she needs in her needs being met, she actually becomes vulnerable to the truth of her heart inside of her.

Being a Dakini and Tantric Healer for so many years, my job was to be of service for others, like Mother Theresa, never thinking about what mattered to me or my own needs. It was always about everyone else. And, after making a decision one day after about 20 years of helping others, and working on myself, alone, I prayed out to the universe with a powerful intention that it was my turn to have the love that I helped everyone else so much to open to, and return to me.

It takes a very strong man to have love and a life with a Dakini, who had so many followers, who had been devoted to her, requesting time to be with her, and yet so much detachment from them, separation, and loneliness along the way. And having been so detached myself, not creating any bonds out of being a professional, there was no depth of love in my heart to receive and heal within. It was always about them, the other, giving, but no receiving, and no opening. The amount of openness I could give was then limited because I was not getting what I needed. There was no balance, and all that was left was a waiting, a longing for something bigger, greater, and more profound than I had ever experienced before.

All the training I had received prepared me up to this point. And when I went to see my original Daka Tantra Shamanic Teacher from 13 years prior in May of 2017, and shared with him that I had spent countless hours, days and months with a particular man, and my heart was fully connected to him in heart and in spirit, he did not hear me. He took it as a rejection, as though I was shut down. And yet, I was more open to my true self than I had ever been. And, in the process I felt powerful in knowing I did not need sex from him. All I had wanted was love, and since he was my teacher, and lover from the past, he was clouded with his view that because once I was boundary-less and had the notion of polyamory, that I would remain this way at all times. However, my deep heart opening and expression of this to him, was the opposite of his view. And my only answer was to walk away in this moment, as I was not heard, and my truth was dismissed. This then was the beginning of my knowledge that the man I had spent all these months with, was my one true love, and the man I was going to choose to spend continuous countless hours, days and years with from that moment forward.

After Years of Hard Work, I Finally Found Him

After many years of transformation, healing and a stand for leadership, he walked into my door. And with determination, he chose me initially, but I became a demand he transformed through some recommended transformation programs and commit to the process. And what happened was that he stayed. And he actually did the deep healing work I requested. And in the end, it was I that needed the deeper healing. After having trained him and helped him heal for almost 2 years, it was my turn to heal. And after much resistance, I surrendered.

So, I Finally Have Him, Now What?

When you've finally captured the man of your dreams, in being a Healer, having the wisdom, knowledge and education to train him to be a Healer, in numerous modalities you learned, he then can help you. However, being a Healer for 20 years and a man in training for less than 1 year, there really is no comparison. However, if he is a willing man, has fully chosen you, and is committed, his gifts can only get bigger, better and stronger in time. He must be willing, interested and desire to learn, desire to be educated, desire to learn everything he possibly can, and everything that resonates with you. And, ultimately as a woman, you too, must be willing to try out some of his recommendations. There must be a balance, so he feels the equality. Nevertheless, after you've both explored each other's recommended paths, the time will come back to working on the woman, who in fact is the one who had the past rape(s), or child birth(s), or lack of love from the past. He will get his turn too though. That is not to be dismissed.

So, what do you do when you've found him?

How do you keep him coming back? How do you know if he will stay by your side for the long term and help you heal, truly heal?

The one main reason I knew my man would stay is the level of respect he gave me in those initial 9 months we knew each other, the level of honor, humbleness, kindness, follow through, commitment, willingness to listen, to be vulnerable with me, and dedication to his own journey of personal growth. There was a common theme that showed me we were meant to be. One in particular was the similar background, of love, from childhood, a similar degree of personal growth, similar commitment to personal growth, and a similar desire for true and lasting love.

Also, there were numerous signs that kept coming to us to show us there was something about our connection unlike anything I'd experienced before. My birthday and the street number he grew up on, the same. One of his best friends' names was almost the same as my ex. His birthday was the same as my ex. He found me through my tea site and brought tea on our first meeting. One night after months of knowing each other, we decided to go out to eat, and on our way home we found a $20 bill on the ground. That to us was a sign of good luck to come! My son had similar behavior and education issues he had to get over as a child. He loved the mountains more than the beach, as do I. He loved to write and journal, as do I. He loved to talk, even more so than I. He loved talking things out through communication, as do I. He loved eating out, travel, Shamanic Journeys, children, beauty, and being social. His mom and my mom both love golf! And, his mom and my mom, in fact are like sisters, so much in common.

Training Your Man to Heal You

When something has come up for you to heal, and you're in a serious relationship with a man that you love, it is super beneficial to take the opportunity to be able to provide Healing for each other, given that both people are willing to be coachable. When it's you as a woman that needs the healing, *Teaching Your Man to Heal You*, then your man needs to be secure enough in himself to provide the healing to you. He needs to be willing to take the feedback, requests of moving positions, suggestions of shifting the energy, and not push you beyond your limits. When you've reached your maximum capacity of the energy he is working with, especially when it comes to sexual energy and sexual arousal, he has to understand that you may be healing from old wounds or traumas, and not to take it personally.

Often, when you are feeling vulnerable, and your guard is down, old wounds can get resurfaced, and his willingness to be loving, supportive and understanding is the one thing that will help build your trust in him. And hence, your willingness to be close to him, and continue Healing in your process with him. Otherwise, it may shut you down from him, put up a wall between the two of you, and have you need to go to someone else to heal you instead of him. And when you are married, and love each other, or are very close, the best reward is in loving each other and providing the love each other needs. And when someone makes a mistake, don't make too much meaning out of it. Forgive each other, take the feedback, and try again.

Your Beloveds Clearing After Initiating Him into Reiki

My Beloved felt a whole new relationship with the Divine, God if you will, spirit, and his connection to source and his soul. He felt he was having an identity crisis because it brought him to question his relationship to religion and God. He started questioning his beliefs to his own spirituality and having memories of past lives. He even started having intuitive gifts come to him and when he practiced giving energy healing sessions on me, he would have psychic impressions of my past life experiences that I needed to heal from where he assisted to support the healing of this process.

Usui Reiki Level 1 is about healing the physical body. I spent a good 2 years as a Usui Reiki Level 1 Practitioner back in 1997, when I was first attuned before I attempted to receive the Level 2. Reiki Level 1 helps detox one's physical body. It helps to cleanse toxins, pains, extra weight, releases energy out of the muscles and organs, and there are many days, weeks, and months one may have headaches, go to the bathroom more frequently, have exhaustion, and a physical detox reaction. For this reason alone, I recommend anyone who is interested in going on the path of becoming a Reiki practitioner, to start with level 1, and give yourself at least a year before moving on to the next level. Everyone in our society today wants a fast solution. They want quick results, a fast path to transformation, and to step up and become Healers immediately. However, becoming a practitioner isn't something that can be rushed. One must take their time, so they can process and work through all the layers of their body, mind, spirit, and soul. This process cannot be rushed. Each person's process of Reiki will be different; however, I do not agree with the teachers who have taught students Reiki Level 1 to Master in one weekend. In my opinion, they are only doing that for business and to make money, but not truly doing the new practitioners a service of being grounded in the practice. Just like Martial Arts, Karate, Chi Gung, and other practices, it takes years to learn the foundations and basics before even considering oneself a Master. Becoming a Master of anything doesn't happen overnight. It happens over time, with dedication, commitment, practice, and a grounded understanding of the practice, as it becomes who they are. Everyone has a choice, but I choose to learn and teach things in the old-fashioned traditional way, doing it slowly over time.

Witnessing and supporting my Beloved after his experience of receiving Usui Reiki Level 2 was quite an extraordinary process. I remember the first three months alone; he would be on the brink of tears nearly every single day. His heart was so wide open, and he would go into an emotional release rather quickly after this experience. Reiki Level 2 is about healing the emotional body, and many emotions release out of all parts of the self, the physical body, the organs, the muscles, the energy body, the auric field, the meridians and so on. My Beloved chose not to receive his Usui Reiki Master attunement after 6 months or a year had passed, so he continued working through and processing at the emotional healing level. Anyone who knows him, knew he was so in touch with his emotions and connected to his bigger heart. This was a big part of the why.

For anyone who receives their Reiki Attunement, Slow down, heal yourself, take the time to process, get acupuncture and allow the emotions to release from Reiki, especially Reiki level 2.

For anyone who receives the Usui Reiki Level 2 initiation, it's important to take the time to process the emotions from this attunement, and if emotions are still releasing from your experience, there's no rush to move on to the next stage.

Reiki is an excellent addition to teaching your Beloved how to heal you, in combination with Breathwork, Meditation, working with the Chakras and Tantra. It's almost as if they go hand in hand. Combining Reiki with Tantra is a perfect blend of energy healing, clearing, awareness, and kundalini opening, expansion, and bliss. I don't recommend doing it any other way. But always go at your own pace and follow your own inner wisdom.

After my Beloved Received his Kundalini Reiki Master Attunement – a story

We were in the kitchen of my one-bedroom apartment. I was cooking breakfast for us. It was the summer and we had time alone. He was ecstatic and energetic with a perplexed looked on his face, confusion of what was going on with his body. He had leaned over the counter. I placed my hands on his hips. His body started spiraling. His hips were spinning like waves in the ocean and his erection was as large as it could have ever been. He felt energy rising up from his spine going up to his crown chakra. He was making sounds like a laughing monkey and a happy lion.

I suggested he go lay down, but he couldn't be still. We walked, stumbly, to the mattress on the floor in the main room (I used for massages, energy healing and such). He got on all fours. His energy was still spiraling, but even bigger now that he could close his eyes and lean into the mat underneath him.

I jumped on his back, and put my hands on his shoulders, my feet on the mat underneath him, and I leaned back to help guide him to sit on his heels. He had so much sexual kundalini energy running through him. He didn't know what to do with it. He didn't know how to control it. I said, "hunny, breathe. Take deep breaths. Close your eyes and melt into the feeling."

He said, "I don't know what to do with this. Should I laugh or should I cry?"

I said, "Either works. You're just feeling it all."

He said, "No shit. You're not kidding!"

His whole body went into waves like the ocean. He said, "Hunny, you're my Captain and you're steering my ship!"

I jumped off his back, and massaged his lower back and his hips and placed my hands on his tailbone, then pulled the energy down the back of his legs. I said, "Hunny, close your eyes and breathe. Take really deep breaths, and exhale really slow."

Well, he was out of control. He was so worked up. All I did was gently touch him in the kitchen with my love, my passion for him, and a slight touch on his hips and tailbone, and this is the result. Wow!

I said, "Hunny, it will settle down. Just relax and breathe. You're ok. You're just riding the wave of bliss now."

He laughed and rolled on his back.

I wrapped my arms around him and held him. We breathed together. As he laughed, I felt the ripple of energy run through my body and I laughed right along with him. I breathed to help show him how to breathe, and eventually he started catching on. Eventually, he started breathing at my pace. And after about a half an hour his energy settled down, some. He was a walking laughter and sex bomb around the clock, but his energy had come to a gentler pace after a little while. Until later.

Why is this story so important?

The reason this story is so significant is because when the man you love is vibrating at an incredibly high frequency, and an extreme of kundalini and sexual energy, it will trigger all the unprocessed and unresolved issues his partner has inside of her – that perhaps she never even knew she had. When your Beloved is radiating an energy of love, bliss, and kundalini pleasure and not even trying, it can, for some women, bring their unresolved sexual traumas to the surface. Some couples come together after such extreme initiations, but in this case, they happened simultaneously.

After my sweetheart's initiation, I saw very clearly how whatever was inside of me that needed to come to light, came to the surface to be realized, and we got a chance to work together to release it, process it and integrate it. We created our own style of healing after these experiences, and our own healing modality that helped to assist in the releasing of this process. My Beloved and I created our own method of hands-on healing, energy healing, bodywork and breathing that helped the assistance in allowing these energies to be cleared. So, while he may have been the one originally to receive the Reiki initiations (that I attuned him to myself), I, being the Tantra Practitioner for so many years, our collective knowledge, wisdom and spiritual power brought together a modality that helped the full transformation of the sexual wounds and traumas out.

However, healing all of the layers doesn't happen all at once. Sometimes the giver becomes the receiver for a while, and the receiver becomes the giver for a while. It happens over time, layer by layer. And this here is the story of the beginning. This book will be followed up with a Healing Modality we used and created to assist in the transformation and releasing of these trapped energies in the body. For now, use this book as a Guide.

Making Requests

What does it mean to make requests? How easy is it for you to make requests of your man? Do you hesitate, stall, or give up on what's important to you? Or are you a demand that what matters to you is actually heard, supported and understood?

Communication is the basic tool one needs to access getting a hold of your man's (or woman's) hearing. Without asking, there is no listening. Without making requests, your partner does not know what you need. And if he does not know what you need, how will your needs ever be met?

Making requests goes beyond being timid, shallow and passive. One cannot be passive or insecure in making requests. You must be 100% sure that what you are asking is something you want and need, and therefore, just as confident when you make the request to be heard.

In order for a request to be fully received and responded to, there must be full intention and attention on the request you are speaking of. Otherwise, your partner might not take you seriously, and ultimately, not respect you, or respect your needs as being very important at all.

Intention on Requests

"Your ability to create intention and your ability to be vulnerable is the greatest gift you have." Paavo

Being Intentional on Requests is just as important as asking your Beloved to massage you, hold you, or make a purchase of a new couch or car. Intention is the key that holds the power of what you speak. When my Beloved tells me he desires to cuddle, and requests of me to lay down with him ahead of time, I respond kindly. When my Beloved requests of me to make love to him and tells me he wants to go to the bedroom to be alone, I think about his request and make sure we are alone and there will be no distractions. If it is the right time, we will proceed often in a prompt manner. If it is not the right time, be sure to come up with a new suggested time and an agreement before you separate, or a time to check in again.

Teach Him to Be a Gentleman or Fire Him

Are you a woman who gets into relationships with men who don't know how to respect you, honor you, support you, love you, caress you, or be gentle to your needs?

Are you a woman who tries to teach your man how to touch you and request of how you like to be touched, but your man just simply won't listen?

When it comes to a woman, her needs are especially particular and imperative in being heard. She has her own intuitive feelings and energies that will guide her man in opening her, but if he won't listen to her intuitive messages about how she needs to be opened, he's not honoring the feminine Goddess. And the result is she is not feeling empowered to be a woman to be her individual self, and he's also not getting the beautiful flow of sacred respect back to him.

A woman must be a demand that her man listens to her. If he cannot listen to her sacred needs, he's not man enough for her, period. He's not able to handle her in her power. He's not trusting in her guidance, her intuition, her heart or her love. And in that case, he also is not trusting in himself, his own heart, his own love or his own guidance. There is no foundation of a loving relationship to be built on, and the only option is to **fire him**!

A man must be strong enough in himself to be willing to surrender to his woman. If he cannot, he simply cannot handle a powerful woman! It's not a man's job to dictate what energies, feelings and emotions are rising in the Feminine Goddess. He is not the Goddess, so there is no way he could channel this information for her. She must do it, and she must be a powerful request or demand that he listens to those messages, and in that she will open up like a flower, like a butterfly, a rainbow ready to shine! A man is not woman, and a woman is not man. Period. There are many who argue this case, however, it is what it is.

A man is the powerful force of being grounded, present, and like a warrior knight ready to protect her and love her. He cannot do what she does. He must hear her and let her open to him as the Goddess she is. Anything else, is just hog-wash!

Now every man has masculine and feminine energies within him, and every woman has masculine and feminine energies within her. That's a separate discussion, however, each individual is separate from another. How you feel, how you think, what you need, what you crave, the sensations you feel in your own body are yours and yours alone. No one else can experience what you are experiencing. No one has that kind of power over another, and if they think they do, or they try to, they're only fooling themselves, and the one they are with.

Being a Shiva for the Goddess

"I am blown away how amazing my love making has changed since I have been a student of Asttarte for over six months and now being her beloved, lover, best friend and future mother to as many children we choose to make in the next couple of years."

"First and most important I realize it's my job to honor her each and every time we begin a love making session as my Goddess. In a way I have allowed myself to be the submissive especially as she has been teaching me the art of harnessing our energies and meeting as one."

--Paavo

Now, this never happened (having children that is), but your Beloved honoring you is significantly important for the love to remain and stay strong. For a partnership to stay strong, honoring each other must continue, even after years of being together. Relationships fall apart when the honoring disappears (I discuss this in the book that follows this one: Grieving the Shamans Way; What I Learned from the Love of My Life Dying. Info is at the end of this book.)

How BDSM Saved My Marriage

We had just finished our first Shamanic Journey together. We went to see these Shamans who offered heart opening medicine and Ayahuasca. We never did this before together. The entire time we were laughing and there was no way we could be separated. Everywhere he went, I went. If he didn't stay by my side, I demanded he did. He knew I needed his presence in this experience. I was working on healing my deep core broken heart from my maternal side and the abandonment since childhood. I knew this was my time to finally heal.

If he went off to talk to new friends and mingle with them, I would immediately find him, and take his hand to pull him somewhere we could go in private. I needed his strong body on top of mine. I needed him to hold me down. There was so much energy coming to the surface to be released. And he was my hero, my vessel, my anchor to stay grounded and release what was in my physical body.

We would be down in the basement for a while, my kundalini activated, and lots of screaming. It was a lot of work for him to be my anchor. I was a strong powerful Tantric Goddess who had a lifetime of trauma still to heal. And he just happened to be my Healer; after 8 months where I was his. The roles reversed. Although I was still his Coach. I was still his Dominatrix. That would never change.

After a while, he was getting tired of holding me down. I had been screaming for a couple hours (off and on of course), laughing and sobbing in between. It was a lot of work. Perhaps a lot on his body to use all his weight, pressing into my belly with his fists, holding my shoulders down with his hands, laying on top of me with all his weight, and moving whenever I asked him to, and requested it. So out of nowhere, he disappeared. He went upstairs to get something to eat. Now, I was a Tantric Dakini Goddess who was just beginning to release her lifetimes worth of trauma. Of course, I had many more layers to release. But you know me, I wanted to get it all done NOW. No time like the present.

After the initial shock that he was gone, I took a few breaths, jumped off the air mattress we were laying on, and ran up the stairs. The Shamans there knew me well. They knew my background and the powerful Healer I already was, and they knew what still was yet to be healed, or at least that I was just beginning the thick of it. So, when I went up there, and saw all these smiling faces looking at me, and they all turned to look at him, they knew he was a leader. They knew he was a warrior and that he could handle my intensity, but they also knew he needed replenishment. They suggested I go back downstairs and be alone for a little while, while he ate and refueled himself. I tried this. I layed down for a little while. I tried to rest, but it wasn't easy. So, after fifteen minutes or so, I ran back upstairs to find him. He was still eating, so he brought his bowl down with him. He wanted to finish, but he also wanted to be with me. He was as loyal as they come, and he knew the work ahead of him, and the work we had already done. He was humbled he could assist in this way. He was blown away at the level of commitment I had to grow, and he knew I was his Goddess, and he would do whatever it took to help me achieve my goal of complete transformation.

So, we began again. This time, more subtly, gentler, and moving into it softer. I wanted more pressure on my chest. I felt like there was a huge anchor weight trapped inside of it, and I wanted it out. It was uncomfortable holding onto the karma of your entire family in your heart and feeling it all at once. I was determined to be rid of their pain inside of me, that had become mine over the duration of my lifetime. I knew this work with the Shamans was a key to my breakthrough. I knew my new Beloved was my Master and equal Partner in Healing. I knew it was the time to go all the way. And this one night, this one Journey, was only the beginning of many. Mixing BDSM techniques within the realm of Sacred Medicine, plant medicine and Shamanic Healing went hand in hand for us.

My beloved was in Recovery for Addiction. He had gone through the 12 Steps of Recovery work in several programs for nearly 30 years. He had the tools of addiction recovery and was also still highly sexual, still had fantasies of sexual pleasures, and had come to me as his Healer to help heal his heart with his mother, to help him heal deeper layers of Sexual Healing and Addiction, and I was advanced in the Tantra Healing Arts, the art of Sexual Dominance, and had no problem being his Dominatrix. I also had no problem receiving his direction of healing, love, and submission to opening my own heart. It was a battle of sexual play, attachment to being together, and the struggle of running away from each other and having space and freedom to be ourselves. We got through it. We got to the other side. I'm writing this story 5 years after this first experience. We've done numerous Shamanic Journeys, have worked with nearly all the sacred plant medicines and shamanic tools, and have released each other's karma of our lifetime. This story is my testimony to this powerful work, the testimony of working together as a Couple to heal each other's karma, and the true story of how love can heal anything.

Being kinky, being open to sexual play and BDSM wouldn't have had its power if we had not had all the recovery work behind our belts. It would not have worked if we were just novices, and new on the path of healing. It would not have worked to the degree it did have, had I not been a practitioner of Healing for so many years. It would not have worked if he had not gone through his AA recovery for 30 plus years and the many other tools of healing on top of that. And it would not have worked if we had not done most of the workshops and leadership trainings at Landmark Education, now Landmark Worldwide. For all these tools, we are grateful. And with determination, anything is possible.

Learning A New Sexual Experience, by Paavo

Funny, I have made love many times with my Goddess during the past year. I truly had a point of view that I was not a sexual being. My Goddess has told me on multiple occasions that I am actually the most sexual man she ever met.

The lessons that I've learned over the past year were profound and magical. We even waited four-months of living together before we made love. It was a time to build the heart energy day after day before we made the joint decision to actually place myself inside of her. It made for a hardness and wetness experience like never before for each of us.

When I first had that incredible experience of making love, I can remember that night only that I was Crying while she laid on top of me as I was screaming out loud over and over "Am I going to die? Am I going to die?"

The entire year of lovemaking has been the most-wild ride ever. Each time knowing, I was making love to a real Goddess; a human being can only experience when being taught by the master herself. Many times, she was whispering to me "Don't move hunny. Just feel me."

Only to discover that my favorite position with my beloved is me laying on my back and having her run the show. I can't tell you how many times she would ask me "Please don't move. Let me do all the moving." I could never understand what she meant. How could I possibly be having a love making session and not moving? It must've been the way I was raised that having sex was performing or just doing it anyway without really deeply listening to my partner...*let alone a Sex Goddess!*

Nine days ago, I was placed under the knife by a surgeon who performed a total hip replacement. The physical therapist told us not to have sex until the doctor gave us permission. Most people wait for four weeks. But here I was eight days into recovery and two hours before leaving the high-end Assisted Living facility I had been recuperating in, that I would learn the lesson of a lifetime. We studied the stick drawn diagram of *How to make love when a person has just had a hip replacement.* It was most important that I laid on my back and just pointed my toes straight up in the air. That was all that I was to do.

As I laid on my back and my Goddess placed me inside her, I got the lesson she was asking me to be still over the course of the entire year. My Goddess had expressed to me on multiple occasion to not move. Here, I was told to only keep my toes straight in the air. It was in this incredible moment of laying there and feeling pure bliss did I learn this new lesson of taking direction while making love!

While I was laying on my back and focusing on my toes straight in the air my beloved placed me inside her and the magical gift appeared. When she says "don't move" that means don't move, and Wow, did I learn the lesson of laying there and feeling pure bliss. I lost myself in that love making session; just laying there feeling a much deeper heartfelt connection than **ever** before.

I now know what it means to be still and "don't move" and *damn,* it took me having my hip replaced to learn that lesson. I am forever grateful that I met the Goddess of my life, and I can now start to take directions and really understand the magic of just being still while making love.

Paavo

The Heart On   Asttarte Deva

Wild Tantric Review
~ July 2018

We had the most amazing two days, and at the end of the night after coming home from the most beautiful fireworks, we felt so connected to our love; a reminder of what we mean to each other. We watched the rest of a very intense and dark government movie we both were so into and were left feeling sad for the main characters death. We cuddled and embraced into each other, and I wanted to feel heart love. I was feeling heart love when we laid in certain positions, and when he moved out of pain or discomfort, my connection to the energy of love moved with him. He was so aroused, so electric, so filled with love, and his rock-hard shaft was there waiting for me, but I wanted a deeper feeling of my heart to his heart, and so I waited; patiently. My waiting patiently for that feeling to come caused impatience in him, and so his rock hardness turned soft. And in that I felt disappointment, sadness, movement yet again of where it was to go. He wanted to then move to rest, sleep for the night, and I was still feeling the movement of arousal coming to a peak, and it wasn't ready to slumber. My arousal was there, but it was my heart that had been waiting. I had mentioned to him, "I can wait for tomorrow", but I didn't really mean it. What I meant is, "open my heart, melt into me, and let me melt into you my love!"

As he felt his exhaustion creep up on him, I felt a craving, a need, desire, to raise his energy yet again, and I devoured him. I kissed his ever so soft man cave into my mouth. I opened it to a reminder of his pleasure, kissing his softness beautifully, sensually, liquifying his energy into a solid form of gold. He asked me if he could watch, for the first time seeing his beloved love him in such a way that he cried in tears of joy and gratitude. As he wailed, his heart opened again, within moments, and he expressed gratitude for my ability to take him from one extreme to another, and I asked him if I could please put myself on him and connect to his heart soul in such a manner that we would dance together in the stars of heaven.

As we danced, I could feel his need to make sound, and yet he was quiet, and so I encouraged him, "Please make sounds my love. I want to hear you."

He said, *"Really? It's ok?"*

I said, *"Yes, my love. It will open you more and melt my heart into you."*

So as he whimpered in pleasure, I too, made my animal sounds of joy, laughter, and pleasure. The energy of what we were creating was getting higher and higher, and he said in a moment, "my love, we will one day produce a child, for I will come to you every day until we do, and we will succeed." And with this, my excitement rose, and in a moment of him pulling my hips deeper into him I made my loud tiger sounds and pleasure growls, until I finally peaked my first orgasm. But he continued his movement, and in a moments time, I was ready for my next breath, my next orgasm, as his hands were deeply pulled into my hips. I felt the connection from his hands on my hips, and his love, passion, commitment and intensity mesmerized me, and pulled at my very depth of pleasure. I was about to take my next peak of orgasm, and all of a sudden, he moved his hands. The energy immediately stopped.

I then raised my animal voice, and said, "please put your hands back where they were." And he moved his hands to another completely different area. I felt his shaft getting softer, and yet it was still firm inside me. Then he moved his hands yet again. I asked him again, please put your hands back, on my hips, and tried gesturing his hands showing him where on my body I needed his touch.

He then moved again, and my frustration had built so high and I was so disconnected from the pleasure and orgasm had suddenly disappeared altogether, and in a moment he increased the peak, pace and intensity, and then he came.

I was taken aback. I immediately was filled with a fierce roar that he ignored my gestures, my pleasure, and put himself before me, after numerous discussions that he needs to hold back to strengthen his muscles inside and release his seed only once or twice a month, not as often as he has been. And I was abruptly surprised he would go against what we agreed, that my inner roar turned to an immediate anger and I slapped his belly once, then again, and roared louder. Then I got up and paddled his behind with my hand. I let out my deepest frustration; my inner dragon, my inner warrior, my inner Goddess coming to rise, and I only wished I could cry.

I then asked him if he could please lick me, and with much hesitation he tried, but the energy was gone. We were both filled with sadness; I over hurting him and his seed releasing before me, and he over being hurt, feeling rejected yet again, unloved and perhaps feeling trapped with a woman, in his mind for that moment didn't love him.

And oh I do, love him ever so much, for without loving him, trusting him, honoring him, would I not have had the courage to tell him all my deepest heart's desires, needs, and hungers.

And yet, my heart craved him. My beloved, my husband, I love you more than you will ever know. And I will prove my love to you...every day...for as long as I live!

I will beg for his forgiveness. I will humble myself. I will surrender to what he needs, and in return, I will ask for his patience, and to please kiss me every day; from the softness of the skin on my face, to the wetness and joy of my inner lips.

And all I ask, is for you to stay with me, love me, hold me, and hold your seed as long as you can, so your heart love and my heart love are one!

The Heart On					Asttarte Deva

King of Hearts Quotes

People are often unreasonable and self-centered. Forgive them anyway. If you are kind, people may accuse you of ulterior motives. Be kind anyway. If you are honest, people may cheat you. Be honest anyway. If you find happiness, people may be jealous. Be happy anyway. The good you do may be forgotten tomorrow. Do good anyway. Give the world the best you have, and it may never be good enough. Give your best anyway. For you see, in the end, it is between you and God. It was never between you and them anyway.
--Mother Teresa

The Heart On		Asttarte Deva

Section 2: Healing Her; Being a Shiva for the Goddess

The Heart On   Asttarte Deva

When I Gaze Into Her Eyes

When I gaze into her eyes,
the sun shines through the tiny glass panes.
Spiders busy.
Weaving webs across the outdoor light post.
You can hear the peepers chirping,
mildew across the front lawn
Clouds forming across the sky
Looking like a clown
Glowing memories
Smells
Fears
As I can see her eyes far away
As the time lapses.

--Paavo

The Heart On   Asttarte Deva

Holding the Space for Your Wife or Girlfriend

How do you hold space for your wife or girlfriend? First you want to find out what she needs to feel safe. you want to listen to her, make eye contact. be present with her. She's feeling vulnerable. Be there for her, hold her and just let her feel your love. help her to trust you that you are there for her. Help her to believe you and just be with her, truly be with her. don't have any distractions. Don't be looking at your phone. turn off any other devices or noises. lay with her in bed and just hold her or lay with her on the couch and just hold her.

Practice breathing with her.

Practice eye gazing with her.

Sit with her and hold her hand facing her

When she is ready if she desires offer her a massage

Learn about your partners "Love Language" and be there for her in the way that she loves best.

Writing Letters to Her:

Dear My beautiful Beloved – I am so happy that we found each other. Healing at your core takes dedication, self-love and a partner who can hold space for each other when needed. You are brilliant, a Goddess and an amazing Healer. Time takes time! Nobody knows how far we have come the past few years.

You are my bunny, hunny, and my infinite True Love. Love You Madly, Paavo.

A Man That Loves You

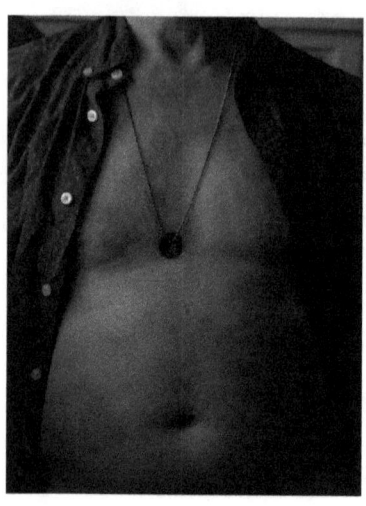

I noticed there was a tightness in my belly, my upper belly. Last night when we cuddled, after two days when I thought I was ready to make love. My dearest Beloved, who has been undyingly patient to connect to me, has been my angel and Healer to no end. I finally tapped a couple days ago on a rape that happened in 2005. Being in casual relationships in the past that didn't last never brought up the deep layers of it. However, being in a long term, committed, monogamous living together relationship surely has.

Have you ladies ever heard of tapping? It's become quite popular and is something I've been doing on myself and offering for clients since around 2001. Go figure, a long-term sex coach who helps everyone else never fully healed from her own rape until stopping her practice for a while and being in a committed relationship. My Beloved gets the prize for being the most loyal and generous man of my lifetime. After an hour or so of tapping a couple days ago, I realized that was all it took to remove the block. However, feeling passion and desire again for your Beloved after so much time where he felt rejected has some wounds needed to heal and forgiveness to take place.

We got together with a girlfriend from France last night I met while living in the old apartment building from years ago. It was quite an adventurous evening with all the kids and running from one park to the next. When we got home it was quite late and was a short trip to the shower and setting my son up for his peaceful evening of sleep. Immediately after my Beloved and I cuddled in the fashion we had the morning earlier. My energy and connection from the morning was so magical. I realized then our love and soul mate connection had never changed, only my own traumas and triggers had surfaced where I finally acknowledged them and processed them. When we connected this evening after 11:30 at night, I felt his intensity of love for me so severely that it hypnotized me and paralyzed me into a euphoria of love that quickly put me to sleep. I felt at peace, at ease, and filled with bliss and love that I passed out.

The next morning (today), he woke up a little triggered, feeling rejected yet again that we didn't make love, however in my mind, we did. We were in the position of making love with our clothes on and the energy between us was more magical than the physical act. We talked it through after his prompts and inquiries of guessing why I didn't want to go deeper last night. At first, I said, "because you suggested we build the energy" like we had in the beginning and feel our feelings of love for each other get stronger every day. He denied that was the reason and asked if I was still in love with this x or that. I assured him, that is *definitely* not the reason. I felt a weight in my belly, so intense that I knew there was some type of emotion or energy there that needed to be released. I remembered how the night before I actually did acupressure on my stomach that brought tears to my eyes right before falling asleep. I knew whatever was in my belly was from some past experience and was something to continue to breathe into. After my son left for his summer program, we had a chance to be alone again.

We went upstairs and he immediately undressed. I matched him leaving on one tank top and pants. I layed on top of him, and we held each other in silence and stillness. I kissed his face, his cheeks, and nose. He kissed my neck and forehead. he had no blocks in feeling his love or connection to me. He knew now that it was my own trauma and fear that had stopped me before. That fear had put a wedge between us, but I wasn't willing to let it take me anymore. Immediately he said, let's get this out of you. There's definitely something big there (Referring to my stomach).

The Heart On   Asttarte Deva

Who I am is the possibility of being loving, of service and generosity.
--Paavo

The Heart On   Asttarte Deva

Healing Your Woman

I sat upright on top of him, and he pressed up into my belly. Immediately I rolled over onto my back. He leaned his body weight into my stomach, using his thumbs for pressure. I pointed to my ribs and right below it. He rotated between his thumbs and then his whole-body weight, putting his whole weight onto me. He's about 200 lbs., and I'm about 124, so it was a lot for me to take. My neck stiffened right away, and I was feeling a small spasm. As he was putting his weight on me, and focusing on my belly, I was holding a pressure point on the right side of my neck. Tears started rolling out of my eyes. I didn't know why. I just knew I needed to breathe into it. Immediately he cupped the back of my neck with one hand and gripped both sides at the same time. The tension, nervousness, and pain there, went away instantly. I found that fascinating how the weight of his body while holding my neck (that always created knots after making love in the past) disappeared while the man I love, trust, and adore was holding it. I heard his words, "You are safe now little one!" And I started wailing. I didn't know what this was about, but I knew this was exactly what I needed.

We went back to focusing on his body weight. He used his arms to alternate between his whole-body weight on top of me, to lessening the weight so I could breathe again. Each time I could take a breath, the heaviness in my soul subsided. I saw images from ancient Native American times, and it looked as though I was in a tribe, and they were performing a ceremony. I don't know if we were clearing a rape from this lifetime, or other lifetimes from the past, as more images from other times appeared in my mind's eye. However, it felt as though we were clearing all the lifetimes of being held down and trapped in a sexual position in this experience, even though we had not even performed the physical act. The almost physical act brought up the pain of the acts from violations in the past, and we realized in this moment, how any exposure to sexual acts, or being put in situations unwanted that were attempted to be sexual or appeared to be had been re-traumatizing for the rapes prior.

For all the Tantrikas out there, and all the Sex Workers and Coaches, I humbly pray for all of you that if you are working in the field, and got there in a way similar as I, I hope you too heal the core of your traumas and receive the love you have been longing for like I have! We all need each other, and now that I have this wisdom after taking time off, and am healing the core darkness, I can help others who have been there too!

For all the ladies who had trauma before your relationship and are with the man of your dreams or someone you really love, there is hope to heal your past and staying in your relationship to heal your pains, get close or rekindle your love again!

I love you all! I love me! And I deeply love you my Beloved Paavo! Thank you for your depth of kindness! It will reap a snowball effect of kindness and healing to the planet! Namaste, AHO, Asttarte

Surrendering to Your Man - A Guide for Women

As a woman adult survivor having overcome multiple violations, child neglect and abuse and growing up not having experienced love, it is not easy as an adult to surrender to others who actually love you. It takes a lot of trust of your man to truly open up yourself, surrender to what's hidden within, and actually let him love you.

What does it mean to let someone love you? What does it mean to truly let yourself receive from him? And if you receive, how receptive are you to feeling it, experiencing it, and having appreciation in return?

When your body is in armor, as mine was after deep womb work, deep scar tissue and birth trauma healing, the process of what occurs to a woman's body after this experience is as though you are birthing yourself to a new you. This is a practice I have trained couples. It is something I have talked about on my YouTube channel, Love Sex and Tea. It is something I like talking about and is the more advanced part of the modality my Beloved and I created together during this time (which will be a Healing Modality Guidebook that follows this one). This is about the stages of healing for other women, and as I express in my couples' blog site, teaching your man to provide this type of deep healing with you (via in person couples work, online videos, my books, or starting just with you).

There is very little information out there on deep womb work and healing female scar tissue. Mostly what you'll find more of is g-spot massage, but I'm not talking about g-spot massage. I'm talking about deep core internal woman's healing, and then what happens after is the energy that was stuck deep inside actually then moves to the outer layers from her vaginal canal; such as the energy moves out to her hips, down to her thighs, and up into her entire belly and stomach area. I've found NO information out there on this topic, and having experienced it first hand, one must be truly brave, willing to go deep with her beloved, and then if deep imbalances show up after (such as hormonal imbalances, gestation development as the body goes into protecting itself, and other deep emotions that can cause havoc until one discovers this is what is going on).

Not knowing what is going on with you can be the worst situation, but as soon as you know, having done SO much deep work, the rest is easy! And surrendering to your Beloved, who had helped you open up originally will be the miracle when he sees you melt back into his arms!

Because after waiting several months while your body turned to ice when all that was hidden deep in the womb finally melts away, and the waiting is finally over!!! Your man is relieved, and you reap the benefits!

Your Man as Your Healer

Can he handle the role? Does he have the knowledge, training and ability to support you in your process? This is the greatest reward in any relationship where your man (or your woman) can support you in your process. It takes a very brave, powerful, strong, and emotionally mature man to handle supporting his woman to get clear in her own journey, her own process, her past, her grief, her own traumas, etc. Can your man handle the job? Is it too much for him? *Your Man as Your Healer.* What can you do to help support him to continue supporting you? Well, it takes two, and in the journey of recovery, transformation, grief work, integration work, inner child work, and healing abuse, one must be very skilled, but also find a way to heal himself so he can be less triggered by her journey. My Beloved likes to use the term, "trigger-less" and claims he is so, but not all the time!

For many many years, I worked in the field of being a single woman, having mainly male clients, and training them how to be loving, gentle, kind and compassionate towards a woman Sacred Sexual Healer, who had been raped, victimized, or in some way sexually been assaulted. Many many women have been sexually assaulted, and far too many that have been assaulted and don't even consider that they have, but they have. And it takes a very brave woman to heal from those assaults, and once she has healed from her violations, the next journey is often healing her inner core self and clear the source of why they happened in the first place; often stemming from mom and dad.

Now that I have an amazing man in my life, and have integrated him into my entire world, I have been training him to be a Healer. There are some kinks to work out and some more Advanced Training to take, but he's diving in head first, and by the grace of God, we are both being rewarded, and benefiting from the journey. It didn't start out with this being the intention, and we had no idea we would fall in love, as these things happen organically, and no one can control who they fall for, but now that we are here, after many many months of healing him, it is now my turn!

So, the journey of him supporting me is a new quest and working on my own inner child is something I had not realized I hadn't done before. As I have been working on my own journey of healing since about 1996, and it has been quite a long time. I had thought I only had one piece left, which was the missing piece of a beloved, but little did I know bringing that piece in would be another HUGE journey of growth and inside healing.

How do you know your man can handle the role of being your Healer? Well, he has to have some experience in healing himself, years of experience would be great (luckily mine has had over 30), but even 10 years would be fabulous! Anything less than that, I wouldn't trust him to help you, and would best advise you to seek a therapist, or other trained professional. However, my guy has been in the role of being of service to others process for a long time, despite lacking the actual training as a Healer. That lack is being filled rather quickly, and the task now is honoring the process, honoring the parts of oneself that need to come out, and letting her speak, dance, write, paint, and play in whatever ways she chooses to! So, here's to a new beginning of self-love, loving another, and letting oneself be fully loved by a man who truly is capable of giving me the love I deserve! AHO!

As he continues supporting me, and I continue training him to help me, I will then be more able, willing and capable of helping all of you!

Much Love,

Asttarte

Women's Emotional Trauma

Many women who live in our society have old traumas from the past. Often these traumas lay dormant in the female body, hidden, and repressed from memory. Some very brave and powerful women have addressed these issues. Some know of them but choose to forget about them. And others have done some healing on them but not cleared the entirety of the issues hiding inside.

When it comes to a woman, it is crucial she goes to the core of her healing process to come out feeling vibrant, alive, powerful, passionate, and fully loved in the world. Even some women who have done enormous personal growth still have healing to do, and even when they have, other layers of gigantic traumas may still impact them for the rest of their lives. However, when the woman, the Goddess, can become conscious of these feelings, these vibrations, these frequencies of energy that hold a feeling, a sensation, or a subtle emotion it can often armor the good feeling and amazing feelings that lie underneath.

The power behind healing women's traumas, is to be fully open and expressed in her need to be loved, comforted, supported, and nurtured. Communication, self-care, personal maintenance and love from others is the ultimate solution to releasing these core emotional traumas.

Hugging a Woman for Healing

What does a woman need in receiving love, comfort and nurturing from her Beloved, to help her heart open deeply to him? Women's minds are different than men. They don't think the same or process the same. However, if they are already sold on their love with you, have already been prepped that you will be connecting through hugging, cuddling, and being held, you won't need to sell them again that this is what you would like to do. Once she is primed, she's already open, and most likely wants your love, comfort, hugging embrace and nurturing. However, if her guard is up, there is something she is dealing with emotionally, she might need that to be resolved before laying down on a bed with you to cuddle.

Most women see cuddling as a very intimate act, so just the idea of it can be daunting if she is not open. You may need to prep her to be open to hugging her before she is willing to lay on a bed with you; even if it is for innocent reasons and the intention is not sexual. Women know it certainly can lead to something sexual, so they want to be sure they feel safe. Women, especially women who have had a history of sexual trauma, don't like to be seduced or manipulated to do something they don't want to do. They want to feel in control, so be sure she trusts you before you try to convince her to hold her. Otherwise, her guard might be up the whole time, and you'll be left frustrated or possibly feel rejected yourself.

Once she is open, she is primed, perhaps begging you or just truly ready to lay on a bed with you and she wants to be held by you, this is when the deeper healing for her begins. You want to show her that you love her and that you are safe for her, and she can trust you, every time she lays with you. This is not about putting on a show and only being deeply sweet and loving the first few times you hold her. She needs to feel and believe that you are a safe anchor she can come back to every time. You want to show her that you are trustworthy, that you will love her for the long haul, and help her know deep inside that you are her true Beloved.

When you are laying together, be sure to ask her how she wants to be held, where its ok to place your hands, and how she wants your bodies touching, or not touching, and the position she requests for you both to be in. Be sure to check in about any physical injuries or pain also. For example, if her neck is tender or sore, or there is any pain anywhere else that might need props for support (i.e. pillows or blankets). Some ladies' ankles may be tender, feet, or lower back for example. Also, if it's close to or during her cycle (her time of bleeding, ovulating, or menstruating), her breasts, womb/ovaries/uterus may also be tender. Be sure to watch for clues or ask her directly if she's sore. She may also not know she is sore until you touch her, so be sure to pay attention and be gentle with her.

Remember, ladies are like delicate flowers, they need to be treated with tender care. Even if they appear to be tough or rough on the outside, on the inside, once they've unraveled layers of their armor, their true delicate selves come out, and their beauty is revealed.

Once you know her boundaries, needs and comfort, then you can relax and truly surrender in holding her. This is when the true healing begins. Healing Cuddle Sessions happen even before you lay with her, but they really begin after you're both comfortable and she surrenders and allows you to hold her.

Once the true holding begins, you can begin to breathe deeply with her. Synchronized breathing is the best approach to build connection, bonding and love and I recommend starting with this. If you both breathe at the same speed and pace, this will help the breath to become synchronized, and ultimately your breath will become one.

Or you can take a follow the leader approach.

Both are tantric in nature, but if you are both being present with each other, and conscious of your breathing, truthfully, this is all you need for it to be considered tantric. As many masters speak of Tantra, as "A Way of Life". There is not one specific practice to follow. There are many practices, styles, and approaches, and all have beauty and benefit to them.

Follow the Leader Breath

An example of <u>Follow the Leader Breath</u> is where one of you breathes, and the other pays attention to your breath, and follows within 4 to 5 seconds after in the same manner. The second person will start the inhale after 4 to 5 seconds (or longer) of the first person. As they are in their exhale, you would want to be in your inhale. As they are in the inhale, you would be in your exhale. Another way to call this, is the *Tantric Breathing Kiss*. You are being kissed with each other's breath, not their lips, but it's a similar energetic connection. You are connecting to the vibration of who they are and building an energy of love.

After your breathing is harmonized, and you are melting together with each other's breath, then deeper healing can happen. I recommend staying in this breathing together for at least 10 to 20 minutes before doing any other practice. Building the energy of love takes time. It can't be rushed.

If one or both of you comes to arousal at this time, and wants to shift gears to orgasmic release, the healing part of the session is over. And, at this point you are truly still at the beginning. Don't rush to end it. You may feel arousal at this time. That is ok. That is normal and may happen quickly or after some time. However, this is a practice of giving a hug for healing to the woman, your Goddess, your Beloved, and there is more to this experience. So, hang in there. Keep breathing. Take your time. There is more to this process.

As the giver to your partner, it is important to be aware of your own energy. You can communicate that you are feeling arousal, however, the point now is to give to her, so continue holding her in your love and be present here. This is the point where you can start to observe how her body is responding, or not responding. If her body is really armored, she may not be responding yet. She may need more time. If she does, that's ok. Continue to breathe with her. You might want to use your words at this point and say things like: "I love you", "You are safe now <u>love</u>", or "You can relax now." This may trigger a response where she does begin to relax. Just continue to hold her. You may want to ask her at this point, "Can I place my hand on your heart chakra?" Or "Can I place my palm on your belly?" Or where would you like me to place my hand?

This is not a sexual practice at this time, so again, don't place your hands anywhere in her intimate parts at this point. If she asks for it, you may be surprised, because she was so armored before. You can then say, "We will get to that hunny, what does your heart need?"

She may make a request of an area on her neck, or her hips. Ask her where the energy feels heavy, in pain, or tight. Continue to stay close to her and try to keep your body wrapped around her while you place a hand somewhere else. Try to keep her connected to her breath. And keep your breathing synchronized as long as possible. This will help her to stay inward and stay connected to what her body is experiencing. If you notice she's losing focus, getting distracted or directing her energy outwards, towards you or talking about something completely off topic, try to hold and embrace her again and bring her back to her breath. If she really needs to share about something, let her finish saying what she needs to say. If she still has more to say, let her finish. You could ask her, "Is there anything else?" Once she's done, redirect her attention back to her breath.

Now we're getting into the nitty gritty of the healing modality my Beloved and I created together. This is one segment of the practice. This work is incredibly powerful for couples to assist each other to release what their bodies are holding onto. The continuation of this practice will be in the Healing Manual that follows up with this book. Stay tuned for updates.

It Takes Two, by Paavo

It takes two persons to work at keeping a love relationship strong and healthy.

I would like to start this article expressing that is has been my experience that it takes two to keep love strong in a relationship. We all know that when we first fall in love how easy it is to stay in that blissful stage, the lovemaking is out of this world and you see your partner as the perfect lover and nothing else. Well guess what, that ain't happening.

I recently fell, deep mad in love and I mean deep Mad in love with the love of my life. I knew in the back of my mind that this would eventually die down and I would be in a situation where I wasn't sure what to do next.

Last December my beloved and I began to do deep warm Yoni massage to try and open her up even stronger. Well guess what happened? My beloved froze and became the "Ice Queen". All of a sudden, she was back into her process. The yoni work brought up old rapes and past dark experiences for her.

I tried everything possible to get my baby back. She was just 100% shut down. The more I tried to change her mind by begging her to make love, she downright would say no! All of a sudden, I found myself slowly shutting down as well.

What happened to that beautiful Goddess who brought me to that blissful love making session no matter how hard I tried I wanted it to go back to the way it used to be. This is why I'm writing this article to share my experience of what I think works to help mend our hearts back together and grow even stronger.

The most important lesson I learned has been how important it is for each person to continue their daily Tantra practice. As well as Eye gazing, breathing, tapping and any other modality that brings you back to your presence. We all need to keep a daily practice with our higher power. When I keep that daily practice strong it is less likely that I will become reactive to my beloved's process. When I shut down, my heart closes and I get back up into my monkey mind and become sad, scared and angry.

It is so important to understand when your beloved is deep in her process. It's her issues and not mine! Once I accept, then I can slowly detach with love and keep my energy clear.

This past weekend my beloved took a trip and it was so helpful to have taken the space that was so desperately needed from each other. It gave me the opportunity to understand that all I was doing was taking on her energy and shutting down myself. It also gave me the opportunity to see that once we were both clear again, we could live our lives working towards all those wonderful possibilities of growing with each other and living a blissful life.

I am going to begin structuring a strong daily intentional meditational practice with myself with my beloved. Because if I don't it will be over, and I'll say to myself once again, love sucks! The next few articles that I want to write about are going to be about some of the daily practices that I learned from my beloved. I know that the love is there, we just we just need to work really hard at getting it back again stronger than ever.

Paavo

"If I don't love you, it's because I don't love me." Paavo

Daka's Orders

So, now he's a demand that I heal,
and after years of being the one who helped him heal,
there's nothing left to do but surrender.

Exercise

Tantra Yoni Chakra Work

To be performed by Husband and Wife/Boyfriend and Girlfriend/ Couples Only

'Must Have Experience in Healing Work and Yoni Work to do this at Home'

Description Below is Only Offered as an Example of Couples Work and Couples Only

Some Background:

After a few months now after the birthing of a *rebirth tantra deep yoni inner walls cervical massage* experience, which I have written some on my women's blog, which was done out of the intention of diving deeper into my own body and gaining the ability to access an even greater connection to pleasure and orgasm than ever before, there's some profound insight to share with the world, actually tons.

The discussion I am wanting to share is in two parts: Part One - the description of the Deep Yoni work.

Part Two: How to Be with a Woman Going through this process and how to help her after (see below called **How To Help Your Woman and Dissolve her Armor and Ice**)**,** and that after doing this deep work, and the impact on a relationship it creates is the purpose of writing and the education on this topic is NO WHERE out there.

The Background of WHY doing such Intense Work:

The Intention Was: to create more feeling inside a woman's sacred center and dissolve scar tissue from birth - The relationship already amazing but wanting to go as deep and close as possible (willing to teach men to do this to his woman in session to those interested in finding out more). **The level of TRUST and SAFETY with your Beloved must be HUGE and already established to do this work.**

Reason: Not totally necessary but having an awareness that a small part of her insides could gain even more feeling - especially when she's tight on the inside, in particular the deep back wall experiencing pain to the touch (especially during sex) or having some numbness there, AND her heart opening even greater to YOU! YES, your wife, or girlfriend opening to loving you even more and falling in love with you ALL OVER AGAIN!!!

Purpose Was: To heal past child birth blockages, deep tightness on the inside of her going as deep as the sides of her back wall, at her cervix, to the left and right of her cervix, the muscles horizontal to her hip joints and upper legs (none of which has anything to do with pleasure and actually only confronts the deepest pain as though re-experiencing the giving of birth to her child all over again. If she's never had a baby, there will be less muscle knots to work out here).

Benefits Initially:

When doing this type of deep work to your Goddess Beloved, can awaken her hidden blocks to pleasure so she can become more fully orgasmic, multiple orgasmic, even if she is capable of having multiple orgasms and ejaculations currently.

Caution:

If she has tightness on the inside and her experience when giving this massage causes her to scream to no end, feel pins and needles, burning and like her leg is going to fall off, pull back immediately and proceed with reiki, energy healing, love, and gentleness intermittently with the deep acupressure on her insides, caress lovingly and hold her in pauses if she cries. ALSO: Make sure you give her orgasms (i.e. g-spot massages or clitoral massages) in the same session or the emotional energy may get stuck and not release fully.

The After Affects and Learning Curve

What may happen and did happen to me, since our focus was primarily on getting the deep muscles to soften, was that for a couple months my body completely shut down. It went through an almost gestation period where my body thought it was pregnant, but in fact, what had happened was that ALL the energy that was stored in the deepest part of my inside, at the ROOT CHAKRA, got stirred up SO profound that all that energy moved to my stomach/entire belly area, hips, and thighs. My body turned to ICE, heart chakra became ice, root chakra, 2nd chakra, 3rd chakra, and so on. And what's so, is that the process of doing another HUGE layer of chakra healing, another layer of body armoring and removal, and the journey to clear the deepest parts of inner childhood, from the ages of birth to toddler years where one first experienced the energy and emotion of love, and attachment to one's first caretakers will be stirred up and needed to process and clear. (The next step of this writing is how to clear armoring and blockages once you've discovered that's what's going on).

Now, this work falls in the Category of Tantra, however, there is VERY little sexual energy that is experienced in this. The majority of this work is to **remove any blockages** to increasing and heightening the ability to experience full body pleasure, intimacy, bliss, multiple orgasms and so on.

Now, I know many of you who have known me for years, haven't particularly known I've been writing on other blogs, working on finishing a book, and especially haven't known that I've done about 50 Shamanic Journeys of diving deeper into my soul, spiritual being, past life, intergalactic self than EVER before! Now, because of this, I've been willing to remove ANY additional blockages that have been left dormant in my cells, cellular body, spiritual body, inner child from childhood traumas and the like. This may be better suited as a chapter of a book, but I'm here, and so shall it be!

So, many of you sexually frustrated men who are seeking to have deep pleasure with your wife, girlfriend, or casual lovers probably might not understand that YOU have to do your deeper inner work in order to have your woman surrender to the depths of being able to give her such a profound type of healing and **FULLY TRUSTING YOU!**

The next stage of this process is **How to Help Your Woman and Dissolve her Armor and Ice:**

The first step is: Is She Willing to Admit she's Armored? Is she able to say, "I don't like this feeling and I know this wasn't here before?"

How To Help Your Woman *and Dissolve her Armor and Ice*

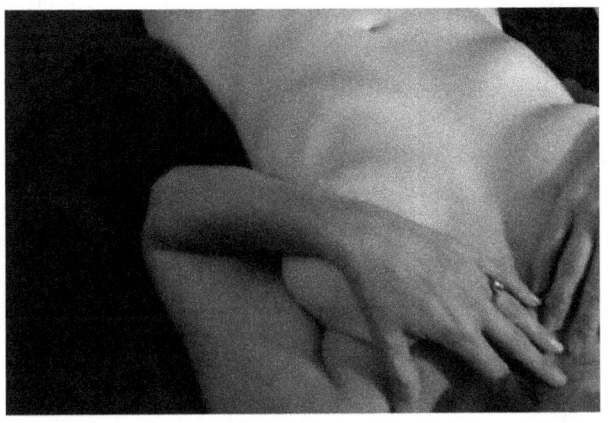

How to help your woman and how do you help her remove her armor and ice, anger, and pent-up feelings?

Are you in a relationship and not getting your sexual needs met because your wife or girlfriend is dealing with something emotional, she's withholding from you, not sure what she's feeling, or repressed in some way?

Has the woman of your dreams changed since you fell in love? Is she different, more quiet, angry or distant?

Do you find it difficult to talk to her and get to the bottom of what she's dealing with?

Do you find yourself daydreaming of how it used to be, or wish things could go back to how they were before?

What if instead of you seeking to find the answers alone, you found the answers together, and grew closer together slowly over time AND resolving the issues of the past so you feel closer than ever before?

What practices do you do together now, and how willing are you to add more weekly practices into your schedule to allow for a breakthrough and transformation?

What if I told you they could, and all it took was BOTH of you being committed to getting to the bottom of it? And all it takes perhaps is the two of you to come into seeing an Intuitive Tantra Shamanic Healer and Sex Coach to help you resolve these matters?

After being in private practice as an Intuitive Healer, Shiatsu and Thai Massage Therapist and Tantra Relationship Sex Coach since 2001, I am now committed to working with Couples to help the BOTH of you come closer than ever before. Some male clients who I saw in the past often would come looking for some sort of relaxation, stress release massage, or think their time with me of an escape to ignore their problems. However, those who came to me that actually wanted healing and transformation of their relationship actually produced those results, and they often didn't need to come to me anymore. We caused miracles, created magic and their hearts opened and healed and their love for their beloved sky rocketed. Love had returned.

However, my mission is a culmination of all my years as a Practitioner, to help not only the men, but also the woman of the relationship, AND the relationship as a whole. A man can resolve matters on his end, and feel better for a period of time, but when the woman joins him in his quest, or vice versa (the woman starting to see me and then bringing her man with her after), this then is when true miracles can happen.

What if the goal as a man is to truly help his woman, and the goal of the woman is to truly help her man, then an infinity happens, and true growth, healing and love blossoms? When the partnership works as a team, is not one sided, each are looking out for the other, each knows themselves, knows what they need to heal within, and is accepting, supportive and honoring of what their partner needs to look at, address, and heal, the relationship stays intact and awakens an empowering context of truth, wisdom and love.

What if you've tried to heal your relationship? What if you feel like you've already tried everything, and you've lost hope? What if you think you already did everything you possibly could, and you are about to give up? The only determination of a relationship failing is when you have stopped trying; when you have walked away and chosen for yourself alone that you've had it.

As long as you keep the faith, open your heart to prayers, an answer, a solution of magic or healing, will this then happen.

The Heart On   Asttarte Deva

Wild Tantric Review

And when you're on top of your man and you are bringing him and are guiding him where to put his hands on your lower back to get a better thrust, and deeper pressure, to hit your clitoris and your buttocks and womb then what you would like to do is to tell him to lay still, hold me tight like a strong powerful grounded man. Don't push me cause when you push me, I lose my energy. I lose the connection to my arousal, my pleasure, and my kundalini link in my physical body. When you're on top of your man and you're coaching him what you want, and need, and he wants to honor you as the Goddess, and you are bringing him to your height, and his height, and both of you are at your peak of Bliss. But you're frustrated because he keeps changing your course of movement when he tries pushing you to move abruptly on top of him, when that is NOT what your body wants to do.

A minute later I go to my closet and pull out my whip. As soon as I know that he is going to try to force me forward or back or move quickly or quicker than my body wants me to go, I grab my whip. I slap his leg or his hip and tell him he needs to pause, stop, hold firm pressure on my hips, or lower back, or wherever my body is asking to be held and grounded into myself.

When I'm ready to slap my man and assert that he needs to stop immediately I slap, and I slap again until he gets it. And he too is filled with pleasure over my power and my dominance and my stand of my love and passion for him. He then knows how much I want him, how much I need him, how much I desire him and how I will not stop for anything in this moment but to grab his ultimate attention and desire and lust for me that ultimately is our union of secret intimacy, blissful love, and desires of a lifetime of love.

The Heart On   Asttarte Deva

The Heart On   Asttarte Deva

Don't look at others, look at yourself.
And let what is inside of you come out,
whatsoever the risk. There is no greater
risk than suppression.

OSHO

The Heart On	Asttarte Deva

Section 3: The Love Cock

The Heart On   Asttarte Deva

The Love Cock

For the Woman
We are all trained for shame around sex. Men come into their connection to sexual activity feeling most often as though they need to perform or be of service in some way. They often want to make love right away, or have sex, however you wish to call it, and be inside his woman when he feels his hardness. But when it comes to a loving relationship, and coming into the sexual experience with love, his hardness is not something that needs to be utilized immediately. It actually produces more healing for himself and for his woman when he can keep his hard cock, and hold her, lay with her, cuddle her, whether clothes are on or off, and be outside his woman. She can feel his commitment, his intensity, his passion for her, and yet she can feel safe knowing there is no expectation for anything to happen. This experience produces a lot of feelings for both the man and the woman, and for the woman, it can create miracles of healing, energy opening in her body that has been blocked or shut down, and especially for women who have been raped or had child abuse, it can create for them the first time in experiencing true love.

For the Man
This experience of the man with the *love cock* holding his woman, may too be the first time in experiencing the receiving of his love and begin to start to believe in himself as a man, at his core; not on the outside exterior ego. It may be the beginning of feeling his power, trusting himself, and also trusting her. He may at first feel embarrassed, nervous, shy, or shame around having his hardness near her, and think he needs to either make love to her right away, or think he is wrong for being hard and tell himself he should be soft. However, this is only him wronging himself, and the furthest from the truth. Albeit, he will still feel so much emotion, and may feel sadness, anger, or fear when this first surfaces, but over time he will begin to accept himself, love himself and believe in himself as a man, with more power, acceptance and freedom.

Men have always been taught from nothing. No one has ever taught a guy about sex or how to have sex. They think it's about how big he is from going to school and talking to the boys in the locker room and if he can give her an orgasm from what he sees on tv, but it's not about having sex right away, or how big he is. It's about loving her. Once he can slow down and let her lead by when she is ready to make love, he will melt into her, and she into him. It's about knowing how she feels inside herself, and when he can meet her where she is at, to feel safe to unravel her pain. Most women have had a background of abuse, rape or some form of trauma, and because of this they often have desire to have sex thinking that's going to make her feel better. It's actually best that she waits, build her heart connection, feeling at one with him, and he is feeling at one with her. It's not about who's right, who's wrong, or sexual frustration, it's about feeling what's underneath the sexual frustration, and getting to the heart of the impulsivity, passion, urgency, and desire. The true connection comes from love.

The Angry Cock

It might sound funny, but it is exactly what energy radiates from someone's shaft if he himself is angry! I don't mean being angry in one moment either. I mean, if his over-all personality, energy and mood is the majority of the time filled with anger, frustration, resentment, annoyance or even sexual frustration. When a woman goes to massage a male's genitals, however he is feeling on the inside, his deeper core emotions, his cock will feel the exact same thing!

The energy of a man's cock will take on the energy of his entire self. And, if he is desiring to connect with his beloved, she too, will feel the anger radiating off of him. She will feel his annoyance, and frustration, his impatience, his neediness, and overall anger beaming energy right off of his sacred area, in addition to his heart chakra, and everywhere else around him.

If his energy is angry and filled with these emotions mentioned above, often times a woman won't want to connect with him, or will have a difficult time, because that energy is not a welcoming feeling. That energy actually pushes people away in the opposite direction, probably the opposite too of what he wishes they would do. An angry cock feels toxic, heavy and the opposite of loving; exactly what women desire to feel. And, if he is trying to connect to a woman, the best way to go about it, is for him to clear his angry energy first.

How Do You Clear Your Angry Cock?

The first step is to acknowledge that you might be angry. Even, if the majority of the time you think you are pretty peaceful, consider, that its possible your energy is not as peaceful as you think.

It's possible that your cock is not angry, however, it still may have stress-filled energy around it that is causing the people, or person, in your life to have a certain reaction. And, even if that reaction is that she cannot orgasm or orgasms very little, that too is an indication that your energy is not as pure as your lover needs it to be.

Instead of blaming your partner, for instance your girlfriend or wife, look within.

The next step after acknowledging that your cock, and whole energy being, might have a certain frequency that is causing women around you to have a certain reaction, is to do your personal work.

How do you do that? The term processing might be overrated, but that's one practice that is helpful. Find someone to talk to about your feelings, get it out in the open, and stop trying to deal with the stuff in your life all alone!

The next thing would be to take on spiritual or peace inducing practices; such as meditation, yoga, tai chi, chi gong, acupuncture, walks in nature, baths, drinking tea, etc.

Beyond this is to get a massage, but not just for the sexual frustration; the whole gamut! Get a massage, or energy healing session to release pent up energy in your entire being; your neck, shoulders, chest, back, hips, thighs, calves, hamstrings, arms, hands, feet, ankles, etc. And, when it's time to remove pent up energy in your genitals, do it with consciousness, not with any intention to release an orgasm (not for a while at least), and remove any blocked energy of anger and stress around your shaft.

There are pressure points, and meridians that run through your whole body, including your shaft. And there may be energy pockets and energy bubbles that your shaft is carrying that is holding stress, trauma, and other emotions. Having the support of a gentle healer to help release these will also help release these energies that your beloved may be feeling. Of course, you can train her, or have someone help train her with you present. This is not about the orgasm when clearing this area, it is about clearing the heavy energy. The orgasm will come, but it comes later.

This section is not just for women guys! It's for men to truly get your woman and help yourself so that you can clear and open yourself to be a match for what she desires; the authentic loving you she desired when you first met, those many moons ago!

So, clear your energy and your cock feels peaceful, loving, and ultimately *sexy*! Isn't that what you want your loved one(s) to feel from you anyway? :-)

Why is it the men are always sexually frustrated?

I would like to elaborate on this a little bit and fill your minds with some perspective that might not have been considered, or perhaps give you something to contemplate for a while.

Women grow up as young girls, and often as young girls we are extremely sensitive to the things around us. We as children are more open, intuitive and feel more intensely what we do as adults. We feel like Healers do and have higher perceptions of things around us.

Young girls often go through life, having to defend themselves, fight off people who cross their boundaries where they feel threatened just for being soft, feminine and girly. These young girls are easier prey to those bigger than them and get picked on easier and sometimes, although not wanted, the worst-case scenarios, we get raped. And, often times all of these things that happen to us, get ignored and many times forgotten.

These girls go through life as if nothing ever happened. We live, we move on and we survive. But yet we have deep hidden pains inside of us. As young girls we aren't aware that we were damaged. We have strong wills and like to have fun. As young women, we express our sexuality and party all the time. But as adults, as fully integrated women, it catches up with us. By this time, we are married, we have children and are fully into our careers. Our husbands don't know our pains. Our boyfriends can't understand, but we know, deeply!

Then it dawns on our husbands that they want more sex. They are frustrated. They aren't getting it, and inside, our hearts are broken. Women are often SO suppressed that they aren't even in touch with the pain inside of them. Sometimes they are, but don't think it's possible to heal, or worst, don't want to. We need to be nurtured, loved, caressed, and cared for as a Goddess and fully respected as women. We need to take the time to open our hearts and expand the flower that we were meant to be. But the husbands we are with are frustrated. They are impatient, and they want instant satisfaction. And, they aren't getting it for the exact reason that their adrenaline is high, and their patience becomes thin. They become demanding, needy and pushy. And as women we see this as a turn off. We pull away. We need safety and aren't getting it. We feel threatened and unloved, and the distance between the two of us becomes larger. Eventually the split from heart and body takes place and sex becomes not something of intimacy or love, but of need and often demand.

And a lot of you men out there are wondering why your wives aren't horny! Well, we women have been through hell, and YOU need to become our Healers, or we will put up a wall from you. So, my dear gentleman, I am here to tell you and teach you, you MUST become a gentleman and give your women the nurturing and the heart of yours she fell in love with. Otherwise, distance will prevail and overshadow any potential relationship you have.

My wish is for all men to learn to listen, to hear what the women of the world truly need and to open your hearts to love them. This then, is when the women of the world will TRULY give you ALL the love you ever wanted!

Blessings to you on your journey!

Asttarte

When You Get Involved Out of Sex

Sex can be an addiction if the intention to connect to someone starts from a place of high sexual energy and the time to build love energy doesn't have a chance to grow. It can create an infatuation with the wrong person. You've already gone through the courting process. You already know what he's like. He's on good behavior right now. When you're the one doing the seducing, you get the wrong guy.

Be kind to others and they will be kind to you. No one owes you anything.

It's just a pattern of addiction, chemical hormones. Getting attached out of sex gives you a relationship based on sex. Getting attached out of friendship and love gives you a real relationship, *bottom line*!

How to Use your Love Cock Instead of Your Angry Cock

Being intentional about being a channel of light, love and healing is the best way you are going to put the energy of love, light, and healing into the energy of your partner, lover, or female counterpart. Even when you think you have perfectly beautiful energy, unless you are a Spiritual Teacher meditating all day every day, or practice mantras around the clock, or a Yogi who lives amongst the Siddhas in a Temple somewhere, most likely you have some energy to clear. Even Master Yogi's and Meditators still have energy to clear, so just remember, sexual and love making energy is transferred and you always want the energy you are going to be sharing to be pure and of light. The best way to do this is with a spiritual practice, energy healing and massage, meditation and cleansing of your soul.

When you are in an intimate encounter with your partner, begin your practice with an intention, creating a sacred bubble of light and love around you, start off with a loving meditation you share together, and do some tantra practices for increasing the love and bliss energy.

Maintaining the Love Cock through Semen Retention

The most common thing for men to do when they feel arousal, is to release the pressure. They will usually masturbate right away, or find a partner to make love to, and help them to orgasm right away and release the pressure. However, as mature men in our society, or men who wish to become mature, they can in fact transform from holding their arousal, and they can help transform their partner as well.

When I say transform in this context, I truly mean transform. When arousal is present and you're with someone you love, or someone you trust, holding in your semen, and breathing into the hold, can help release emotions trapped in your body. Many emotions may rise during this process. You never know what emotions may be on the surface to come up, but for men, when they retain their ejaculation, and hold their semen in, whatever is on the surface for them to process often will come up to heal.

This is how a man can maintain his love cock, by holding in his semen 'white liquid', or 'liquid light', and instead of releasing it as soon as it arises, pause, and wait. It at first may be extremely painful. It may be incredibly challenging to hold in this energy. Your shaft may feel like its vibrating after a while. It may feel like its burning. You may have never held it in before or held it in this long. The important thing to do, is to continue to be present with it, and be witness to yourself and your experience.

Perhaps you may at first feel angry, as feelings of anger come to rise. The anger may remain there for some time, until you process the anger. This is where your loving partner being with you, witnessing you, and holding space for you is incredibly important. Your partner being kind, being a witness, just loving you, without judgment, without making you wrong or withholding criticism, and just loving you during this process is incredibly important.

If you're partner cannot hold space for you in this way, they become triggered with your erection, or they are impatient and want to make love right away themselves, then this practice will not receive the benefits of what's possible. If your partner is also impatient and hasn't done her work on herself to be patient in this process, it may be better to work with a Tantric Healer to help in this way. If your partner can hold the space for you, and be patient, then you both will receive the rewards of this incredible practice.

As the anger starts to subside, the feelings underneath the anger may start to arise. Feelings of confusion, confliction, self-doubt, self-hatred, fear, sadness or other feelings may come up. As you continue the practice with your partner, and are held with genuine love, tenderness, presence and patience, these feelings too will subside. What's underneath this may just be tears; a whole lot of them. You may not know what to do with them, where they came from, or what they are about. The important thing is just to be present to these feelings. The best way to be present to them is just to breathe into them. Let your partner hold you. She may want to rub your back, or your hips, your belly, or your chest, and just hold you from your side. She may want to rub your legs, and continue to assist in keeping your arousal high, but also allow you to breathe into the feelings that are coming up.

One layer of emotion will release at a time. They will not all come up at once, or in one session. This is a process, and it takes time to work through each layer of emotional energy inside of you. As you do, your kundalini will get stronger. Your self-awareness will get stronger. And your self-love will continue to grow.

The important thing to do is to continue the breathing into your body, breathing and pulling in your breath and genital muscles inside your lingham (your male shaft), your anus, and pull the energy up your kundalini channel, up your spine, and pull the energy all the way up to the top of your head at your crown chakra. The exercise seems like simple short instructions, but it takes practice to master. So, achieving all these emotional releases and unraveling of your emotions doesn't happen right away. It takes practice and time, and lots of love and patience.

The hardest thing men could do is to pause when arousal is present, and just be with the arousal. I have witnessed the possibility that this can create and sharing in this story shows the power that this unveils.

The Love Cock as a Path of Intimacy & Enlightenment

The Love Cock practice can at first seem like a tedious, difficult, and annoying practice, but over time with this practice, it can lead to full self-transformation, evolution as a human and with dedication over a long period of time, enlightenment.

There are many teachers who have become masters, with their committed and devoted practice of tantra as the path they took to enlightenment. A couple famous ones are Babaji and Osho. Mantak Chia is also a practitioner of Taoist Tantric arts and became proficient and enlightened in his process, however, he is still living. Working with the energy to retain one's sexual energy and pull it inside their bodies can eventually lead to transformation of the energy centers.

The love cock is a practice that can lead to intimacy and enlightenment because all the blocked energy inside the male body has a chance to be released, with the heightened energy of arousal, and the peaceful energy of love, containment and acceptance, everything has a chance to let go. This is a practice not for the faint of heart. It's not an easy practice, but well worth it.

In order to sustain this practice, as a man, he must be very self-aware, conscious of his energy patterns, and his sexual energy. He must be willing to work with his own sexual energy as a tool for transformation. Only the individual has the capacity to transform himself, and how he feels inwardly when he's alone and with others can be the direct link to his evolution. However, it's what he does in reaction to his own energy that allows for him to expand his energy centers, his breath, his kundalini, and how he responds to his heightened sexual energy when he's around his Beloved or loved ones.

When his energy is expansive, in a heightened state of arousal is the moment he can use his energy for transformation of himself, each and every time he feels his own arousal. The expanded state of pleasure is the energy that can help him to attain an experience of full body bliss, pleasure, and orgasm when he pulls in his own energy and works with it in combination with his own pleasure. The parallel of working with two forces is where the power lies; his own pleasure, charged energy of arousal, and his own breath while squeezing in his sexual intimate muscles (anus and lingham or shaft and scrotum) at the same time, called the Kegels. The breath combined with his arousal ignites his kundalini force and allows for whatever energy and emotion trapped in his body vehicle to be released out of his energy field. There are multiple steps to this practice, and as he retains his seed, and uses his seed to grow his own kundalini, the flower inside of him grows.

I am my Beloveds lover, and as I write this, I share in my experience of witnessing him go through a full body transformation of himself. Men have the ability to transform themselves just as much as women do, however, men's struggle is learning how to work with their seed, and working with their own sexual frustrations, anger, need and other emotions that arousal is showing them. Even Enlightened gurus get arousal sometimes, but they know how to work with and channel their energy to use it for healing and good. Just because someone has achieved enlightenment doesn't mean they no longer experience arousal, but their energy is stronger, more powerful, and they become more aware of the energy they are projecting and know how to use their energy to protect themselves, and use their energy for enlightenment rather than pleasure seeking. Many times, enlightened beings' sexual energy is integrated within their own energy system, so they can then use their whole self to support their loved one or their clients in the assisting of helping them to transform.

Often, where there is a lot of high sexual energy with a person, this is a reflection of how much trauma is trapped in their own bodies. Many times, after sexual trauma, the individual feels more sexual energy than they ever have within their own bodies. This has to do with the imbalanced chakra that had been damaged, overpowered, or violated in some way. Some people will either feel overly sexual from this, or less sexual. This would be a case of needing to heal from sexual trauma, and the love cock, being the partner of someone with this situation, could help assist his partner in their healing. {My book: <u>Awaken to Living; Tantra for Your Whole Life</u> talks more in depth about the chakras}.

Many times, when someone feels a sexual arousal with another person, it usually means that there is a karmic link between the two people and the one who experiences arousal in reaction to the other persons arousal is a direct connection to an intuitive feeling that they are meant to help that person, whether it's as a Healer or a long-Term partnership. The sensation within one's own body when near or connected to another has more to do with the psychic pull to help assist them in their own healing.

The Love Cock as a Path of Intimacy is a practice where the male with the love cock, can hold space for the woman, and help support her to know that she is loved, there is no agenda other than to just love her, being with her, and hold her. And, with his presence, patience, honoring of her and his kindness, her flower starts to melt, the petals start to liquify and open, the gift in connecting to her later is the reward. However, it is not necessary until the link of connection and love has risen and a peace and love has been established.

Do you remember when you were a young child, and perhaps some of you who had strict parents that did not allow you to have sex until you reached a certain again, and you had to wait and just feel love energy with others' years before having sex? That sensation you felt in your body as a child, waiting, wondering, hoping, and feeling pent up or frustrated is that same vibration of feeling bliss and self-love when you wait before making love as an adult, especially when you really want to. That's not to say you can't have sex as an adult. You certainly have the free will to choose to be fully sexual with your partner, however, as a man who is carrying the energy of the love cock it is important you maintain the role of the Healer and be responsible for the energy you are carrying, and how you are assisting your partner in her healing and creating intimacy with her.

When there is an established agreement to hold space for your Beloved in your connection with her, and opening each other's hearts together, taking time to build the love energy with each other is crucial before just jumping in and having sex. The love cock does not exist when you have sex right away. It is only a love cock when his masculine genitalia can be calm, patient and wait before entering her. The love cock practice as a healing practice, is to pause, witness your own emotional healing and feelings that come to the surface during energy play, before sex, letting your tears out, and to allow her arousal to peak, her wetness to expand, and her heart to be fully open before full connection of your bodies. When you wait, it will feel like two puzzle pieces that have been fully placed in the correct position together, all energy centers clear and aligned, all chakras connected, hearts connected, and souls connected as one. When one does not wait to create this container of love with their partner, it will just feel like you're getting your sexual needs met. It's not very fulfilling.

The love cock as a path to enlightenment and intimacy will feel like a reward well deserved. When you put in the work, you reap the benefits, and everyone wins. The love cock is a practice that transforms not only yourself, but everyone that crosses your path.

When the Love Cock Triggers the Woman

When a woman is in the presence of a man who truly loves her, holds space for her, and holds her in his naked body, sometimes this can stir up her own trauma feelings from her past. Sometimes this can cause her to shut down, even when at first, she may have been open to immense arousal and pleasure. Over time, when the honeymoon phase is over, the arousal that once caused her to ignite supreme pleasure and bliss, could lead to her shut down. Her guard may come up, and she may want to wait before having deep intimacy.

For a woman with sexual trauma, seeing her man's hardness, and being held by him, may cause her to have panic, anxiety, or terror. She may hold her breath and not know how to process this. She may struggle touching him further and feel her heart close. She may struggle to look at his nakedness. If this did not happen at first, but arises later, it often has to do with safety with someone she thought she loved, and a trauma from a significant partner in the past. She may not be able to access these deep pains from more superficial relationships that only last a couple years, or if she was dating many men at once. However, after several years of dating just one person, and being deeply held and loved by him, this then may be when the trauma truly surfaces.

Deep trauma from long ago, or very vulnerable, intimate experiences from childhood or early life may not shed their colors with those you have polyamorous affairs with as adults, or those you had been with for a couple years, but after 3 years or more, the deeper truths can be revealed. It can be quite challenging for the man who loves her to witness her going through the process of awakening something that had been dormant for so long and an unconscious memory that causes triggers, ptsd and reactions as though the trauma is in the present. However, the important thing is for the man to continue to be a loving anchor for her, and not to make her trauma reactions even more difficult to process. Remember, she is processing something that had been hidden from her awareness, and it is now up, active, and alive as though it is current and from the present. If you treat her as though you were her original perpetrator, she will then have stronger reactions with you than she even had before.

The important thing is to continue to show her love, shower her with love like never before, and her trauma reactions will lessen over time. However, if you become triggered from her triggers, and react in a hurtful way, the cycle will repeat itself, and she'll only pull away from you more. And, her next partner, she'll have to heal the trauma that surfaced with you all over again. The common phrase known as the trauma cycle will then repeat itself with the next partner and will begin all over again. Please do your best to love her, and if you cannot hold the space any longer to support her, guide her to find a healer to help her with what has come up, so it no longer triggers you, and she has a chance to heal it at its core.

If you are triggered by her trauma, you would best be suited to find a new partner and let her go, giving her a chance to heal with someone that can truly hold space for her, and you the chance to have love with someone else. It is not wrong that you cannot hold space for her any longer. Perhaps it triggers your own trauma, or you don't have the knowledge, training, or experience to hold the space for your lover in this way. Holding on past the point of it being a workable situation for either person is a trap and a sabotage waiting to happen.

The Love Cock is a powerful force that helps assist is healing the woman of her true femininity and Goddess self, but it no longer becomes the Love Cock when your woman who has trauma has to be the one to help you to heal from her reaction. It then becomes a battle of who's trigger is more important, and how much time do we spend in supporting each individual's trigger, and how much time and space is needed for pause in between the triggers. It can become overwhelming and a lot of work and end up feeling like a full-time job of calming down the triggers. This would certainly be the time to take space from the relationship altogether, to give each other a chance to truly process from all the feelings and energies that have come up.

A woman's trauma cannot be rushed to heal, and often ptsd can be a lifetime experience. If the relationship becomes too overwhelming, it may no longer be a match. It's important to come to acceptance with this, and walk away, even when the love is profound and had been something you spent your lifetime waiting for. There will be love again, and sometimes, with space and time, two lovers can return to each other again.

The Heart On   Asttarte Deva

Section 4: An Intimate Exploration to Healing Her Trauma with the Love Cock

The Heart On   Asttarte Deva

Exercise - Day 1

After months of having your heart guarded, with your devoted Beloved by your side, it takes extraordinary selflessness and love for your partner to hold space for you.

I was so not ready to make love to my Beloved, but it had been months where I didn't feel open. And I knew there was a block inside of me. When you have trained your Beloved for over a year and a half prior, you know that he is willing to listen to what you need.

He requested I disrobe. This created vulnerability in me. I paused, and felt the resistance, breathed into it, and eye gazed with my Beloved. For a while after we held each other and laid down.

After some time, I accepted his request. I removed my armor of clothing and laid down again on my back. I requested he hand me the oil. I oiled his body and handed him the oil, to oil mine as well, his legs, his belly, my belly, and my hips. After some time of oiling and massaging each other, I asked him to lay down over me. We massaged each other slowly with our belly's, our legs, the oil and our breath.

After a short time, he put himself inside me. I laid there, feeling trapped, unable to breathe or move, but knew it was my trapped emotions that made me feel this way, and it had nothing to do with him being over me. After a few minutes of not being able to breathe but a few very shallow and short inhales and exhales, I screamed, "I don't want to feel this pain anymore!"

I said, "I can't breathe!" And I felt it all around my throat. It felt like a harness around my neck, like a huge slave collar around my neck in a locket with chains feeling. I couldn't breathe, so I had to scream. I asked him to do Reiki on the front, sides and back of my neck to help break open this energy. I had attuned him to Reiki a year prior and he had been practicing. When we got to the back of my throat, I turned my head to the side to reach the back and we each were drawing Reiki symbols all around my throat. I was breathing heavily, until I laid looking up again, and looked into his eyes.

He said, "Honey, it's not your fault your mom hurt you. It's not your fault you couldn't save your brothers."

And when he said, "It's not your fault your grandmother changed", I started whaling crying. And those cries, screams and sounds came out of nowhere. They didn't stop for more than an hour!

I had no idea I had grief left over of my grandmother. I had thought my healing with my mom and emotional releases with her over the 20 years was also releasing the sadness with my grandmother, but after this experience, I realized I had them entangled, and they in fact were two separate issues.

Exercise - Day 2

On the second day of being held down by my Beloveds hard Love Cock, my throat wasn't as tight. I noticed a point on the sides of my neck, one small acupressure point on the back of my neck at the base of my cranial, and one small point under my chin, jaw, and the beginning of my throat. Again, we started Reiki there, and it was easier for the sadness to come up since we had just brought up so much the day before.

We started talking about my mom and discovered that she in fact was threatened by my beauty and competed with me my whole life and was more like my sister than a Mother. And my Grandmother actually gave me enormous amounts of love, generosity, kindness, fun, held and comforted me, loved me, nourished me, encouraged me to sing, encouraged me to read and do the best I could in school, and gave me hope in the world when I was very young. And, I saw that it was my Grandmother who was in fact more like my Mother, and the one who really loved me. However, when she moved in with my mom and I, she changed her personality completely. I saw that it made sense how abandoned I felt, and betrayed, because I actually did have healthy love from her, but it changed when she moved in and her personality altered.

After about 25 minutes, I had to continue massaging my Beloveds back, so he could keep his firmness inside me. There were moments when he softened, and I massaged him and kissed him all over to bring him back. And we continued the practice.

I was able to accept that I hadn't grieved my grandmother yet, however, for many years I had thought I had. I started seeing how many things about my grandmother, I looked up to, did similar to, and tried living into what she taught me.

I continued crying, and as my tears fell, my Beloved cried in tears of joy that my heart was opening. He thrusted to add pleasure to the healing and paused when we agreed to wait and melt into the healing we just experienced.

My throat felt less tight, and less painful, and I melted into his arms. We fell asleep together after this for about an hour or so. And we woke up feeling more connected than we had in a very long time.

Exercise – Day 3

On the third day in a row of working on opening my Throat Chakra, it was much easier to move into the practice. I wasn't as guarded. I felt more desire than armor, and my touch melted him everywhere I touched him.

We moved into our sensual position of nakedness, eye contact, and coconut oiling our bodies. It was more graceful this time, however, I still felt tightness in my throat. This time, I felt it in the back of my throat inside the deep of my mouth.

I said, "its still there. It's still there."

He moved around putting pressure on the inside of my yoni, and when he got to one point inside the deep wall of my cervix, I felt the emotion there. I said, "please pause, Right there!"

His hardness and his weight got me in touch with my body's resistance and pain. He was so heavy, and I still felt so much wanting to come out.

I started making weird sounds, weird breathing sounds, like a mouse or a quiet bird, and he said, "I can't hear you!"

I made my sounds louder, and louder and louder until I felt the emotion of sadness come up and up.

He said, "tell me how you feel."

I started talking. I wasn't sure how I felt, but I used descriptive words until I got to what I was really feeling; "sad, confused, scared, disappointed, angry, misunderstood, unloved, stupid."

He said, "when your grandmother moved in, she saw how much pain your mom was in, and she couldn't deal with it, and she took it out on you. Your mom took out her pain on you. You were the young beautiful girl, who looked so much like them, a younger version. You were Cinderella."

Then I started talking about how I dumped the bottles of liquor down the drain and my mom then kicked me out for three weeks. He asked me where I went. I shared, "to my dad's house."

"What did you do when you got there?" he said.

I said, "It was fine there, but the house was a mess. I couldn't take how messy it was, so I went back. But when I got home, my room had been completely changed. She destroyed all my paintings and murals I had made on the walls. She covered it over with white paint like I didn't even exist. She got rid of any evidence of me being there." I again, started whaling crying from this. I had never talked about this before, with anyone, and all this old trapped emotion came out of me.

I said, "she's so detached. So emotionally distant. She's always been that way."

"It's narcissism baby. It's who she is." And he held me.

We moved to lay down again and hold each other to ground and settle the energy. I massaged his belly, his hand, and his inner groin area, moving at a pace like a jellyfish, and using reiki to pull out any energy that was stuck.

He said, "Oh my God! You're a magician! How do you do that? You're like from outer space." And he moaned with pleasure that his heart was melting, and he felt me deeper than he had in a very long time. We then fell asleep together for some time, holding each other in this love.

Exercise - Day 4

After 4 days in a row of opening up my root chakra, being held down by my beloveds love hard sexy cock, amazing firm body, neck, arms and shoulders, and opening my throat, I was more open than in a very long time. I still did not want any movement or thrusting, however, I wanted deep kissing. And then moved into some slow thrusting. The penetration no longer hurt me, but it also did not arouse me yet either.

As my request was granted, he kissed me more passionately than he EVER had! I never felt his love so profoundly, so deeply, and so amazing! I exclaimed, "I feel your love honey! I really feel you!" And felt myself move into being vulnerable with this awareness.

He said, "You can feel me?"

I said, "Yes, I really can!"

"Finally," he was overjoyed with amazement, as he felt my connection and that I truly had been open to him as like the beginning honeymoon phase of our relationship nearly two years prior.

He laid over me, and his weight felt like a big blanket, a big teddy bear, and I didn't want him to move.

Exercise - Day 5

We found some points on my inner groin area, my inner thigh, at the top where the ligaments and nerves connected to my hips. The bubble points released heat that traveled down my legs. It felt like huge emotion was there that had been trapped my whole life, a sort of armor of protection that kept my yoni separate from my heart, and I could not feel as fully as I knew I was capable.

A few days before we did acupressure in this area as well, and at that time it felt like a huge Volcano had erupted out of my legs coming all the way down and all over my legs of heat, anger, sadness, fear, and protection. This day, the heat was less, but still impenetrable with intense emotion of being trapped since a young child.

After some time, we began the practice again. My hot red wetness welcomed him in. We laid a towel down, and he hovered over me as before. I kissed his neck and shoulders all over, while he held his weight as to not drop his entire frame on the light of my ribs, chest and waist. I gave him permission to thrust, as I knew he had been waiting, and my body was wide open for it. However, I still was not at a point of feeling orgasmic, or close to pleasure. We were still in the healing zone and there was no rush for it to be anything than this. I felt a point on my belly to the far left, at the waist, a point on the corner of my shoulder, and two points on both sides of my middle back. Having him hold all points at once while also being inside me, holding up his weight and feel relaxed was like asking him to be a magician. He held two points while I traveled back and forth between a few others. We were like Master's concocting a surgery over me of massage and acupressure while making love. It was funny and ridiculous and amazing all at the same time. And I found myself laughing when we both let out a sigh when we took a break to rest.

The points were still speaking to me in a spasm and yet not quite ready to let go, so we put awareness there, as he temporarily pulled out of me.

We eye gazed for what seemed like an eternity as my eyes slowly began to tear. I was content to stop the practice after this and rest into his arms. It felt magical to have my man back and feel him more than ever before!

The Heart On   Asttarte Deva

Section 5: She Healing Him

The Heart On   Asttarte Deva

Shakti's Orders

When you discover you regain your power when the roles reversed, you became the Leader again in Healing him, helping him, and stopping him from working on you all the time!

As a woman in relationship, we know that we need to have balance. In order to feel whole and complete, the giving and receiving needs to take turns. There's an ebb and flow in relationship, and when your man has been giving you healing for a very long time, it can often cause you to feel so much like the submissive, that you revert into child-like behaviors, such as: the little girl syndrome, feeling like a victim, feeling powerlessness, feeling timid, afraid, shy, shut down from your expression, quiet and wanting to be alone, not expressed in the world, inadequate, small, not good enough, and revert back to the feelings you had as a child with your parents. You then become like a child to your Beloved and there is no equality. He then steps into almost a father-like pattern always saving, fixing, and recusing you. But perhaps this is NOT what you want!

So, STOP it! Make him stop it! If he is causing you to feel these things because he is dominating all the time, open your mouth, and tell him to back off, stop overpowering you, and let you have a turn!

When Your Man Resists You, Resists your Power, Your Coaching Him, Guiding Him to work with you, and doesn't want to heal himself

When your man resists, it may look like him not responding to your needs, taking it personally when you tell him not to touch you, or creating a new trigger in you so that he then becomes the Dominant in helping you again.

When it's your turn to help your man heal, and you yourself are also still healing from past traumas, but you switched roles, so you can feel in your power again by affirming your boundaries, making requests of him to ask you before he touches you and this brings up vulnerability in him. It's his turn to actually heal! But when it's his turn to heal, the focus needs to stay on him. When he then does something to trigger you into your old trauma, after a short time of working on him again, one might call this an unconscious behavior for him to avoid being vulnerable with you. In fact, he may use this to go back to being the "fixer", "healer" and "Dominant". Because it's too painful for your man to look at himself. This then will give him the step up to help you again, when in fact, he knew it was his turn and he manipulated the situation to re-trigger you into an old trauma, so he could in fact not look at himself.

Perhaps he did not intentionally trigger you. However, he knew certain behaviors would cause a charge in you, a reaction, or even anxiety or panic. He would then know if it's his turn to avoid those behaviors and not cross your boundaries when it's his time, and you asked him to be sure he asks you before crossing any lines. Perhaps he has trouble with boundaries. Maybe he feels entitled, like he owns you and can touch you, and pull close to you whenever he feels like it. However, as women, especially with past traumas, we need to be asked before anything to feel ok, to feel safe, and to feel in our power.

Helping the Woman by Healing the Man

"I'd like to start this chapter by first saying as a man in our society, the #1 block from allowing ourselves to open and be loved is our ego. Once we have spent over 30 or so years on the healing of oneself…It brings up to the place where we can begin to sit back and sit in the passenger's seat."

"So, as I slowly and reluctantly go towards that seat, I will begin to unveil the armor to let go and start to understand your woman and how important we need to help her heal." Paavo

The only way a man can fully unveil his heart and expand himself to receive love from his woman is first healing himself and being vulnerable and willing to submit and surrender. And, once he is open and clear, he can then support his woman to do the same.

Each partner in the dynamic must be willing to surrender to the other. Many women say it's the men who are less evolved and need to heal. And many men have their stories and experiences and feel the women just want to be in control and are unwilling to look at their deeper selves. As a woman writing, my experience is that men who suffer the most when dealing with their unwilling partner who does not want to do the work.

However, it can go both ways. In now coming to balance I see the perspective on both angles. Women often fear being vulnerable with the men, and men often become angry and frustrated that their women are unresponsive. So, it's all about language and communication. The communication hurdle needs to be overcome and the willingness to talk in full length to get to the source and come out on the other side becomes #1 priority and the source to most obstacles.

The real truth is it's all about timing. If one partner has needs that are not being fulfilled because they expect them to be met on their timing, but his partner needs to go at a different pace, they may in fact interpret it as though they are not being loved, rejected or worst-case scenario, abandoned. But the truth is one partner needs to open slower, gentler, and with more presence, calmness, and tenderness. Miscommunications can happen when the speed and pace of each other is met at different paces. It is best to try to sort out these differences early on, or it could become a problem with maintaining intimacy later.

The Forbidden Fruit

A woman's breasts are an extension of her heart chakra. The most important thing when it comes to a woman's breasts is to know that this is a very sacred part of her body, and when a man is drawn to touching them, to know that a man is seeking to receive love from her heart, a woman's heart, and most importantly, the deep longing they have with their own mother as the young child he once was.

When a man seeks a woman and is gravitating to her breasts, he is actually looking to feel that deep love he felt from his own mother as an infant. When he wants to touch her breasts as an adult, it is crucial to first recognize her as a Goddess, a woman, and the feminine energy she carries.

A woman's breasts lay at her heart chakra, near her breasts bone, at the center of her heart center. And when he wants to hold her breasts, touch them, feel them, and caress them, his desires are to be loved at his own heart as well. A woman's heart chakra carries within it the wisdom of a deep love for the Divine Mother. When you're in a partnership with a woman, take the sexual passion out of your mind, and know that her heart will heal you more than any sexual passion you have for her.

To receive the deep heart wisdom from a woman, it's important to ask permission from this divine being, and make the request of her to be close to her. You don't have to be sexual in order to receive the love from her that you deeply need. In fact, receiving love from a woman, is all a man ever truly needs at his soul level, to heal his own heart.

The desire for sex often is where a man leans into and leads from, however, her heart is what will help him melt into him own heart so that he can evolve and expand into his own full potential. A woman's breasts are what my Beloved calls, "the forbidden fruit", because a woman must always be asked if he is allowed to touch her in this area. She will guide him to connect to his own heart, by the way he approaches her, asks for her consent and agreement, and upon agreement, he will unarmor his own heart and receive the love he deeply craves.

When a man approaches a woman's breasts, and does not ask for permission, and is rejected, he may feel his own heart shut down and close. In order to receive the love you long for, ask your Beloved if it is ok to touch her here. When you receive a Yes, your whole entire body, heart and soul are filled up. When you receive a No, don't take it as a rejection of who you are. It has nothing to do with you. It does not mean you are not loved. What is means is that it is not the right moment. And, perhaps she needs to feel that you are truly present with her, and when you are not present and do not respect her No, if you keep pushing to touch her in the same moment she said no, it may sting you more than it will expand you.

To avoid feeling rejected, pause and wait. Be patient with receiving her Yes, because if you honor her in this moment, it won't be long where she just might say yes, another time. All women need to be respected with her Yes, and her No. If she always says Yes, she may be neglecting her own essence, presence, and love for herself. But when you can appreciate her No, just as much as her Yes, she will give you the greatest gift in loving you that you ever imagined possible.

A woman's breasts lay at her Heart Chakra. What is the Heart Chakra? The heart chakra, in Tantra Yoga, (and many other modalities), is where the energy is available to receiving and giving love. When the heart chakra is honored, all other aspects of her being are honored as well. When the Beloved can acknowledge her in her wisdom and know when it's the right time, she will respond with surrender, trust, and love. When you can trust her inner wisdom, she will grace you with many more gifts than just letting you touch her at her heart. Her entire body just may melt and open to you, and open more and more with each moment you respect her boundaries.

When women's boundaries are honored, respected, and appreciated, she will give you much more than sexual touch, but intimacy on an entirely soul level. In this way, she will feel fully gotten, heard, and seen as the woman she is, and a Divine Goddess will unfold and become the flower she is.

Hugging a Man for Healing & The Love Cock

What does a man need to feel supported and comforted in cuddling him? Each man needs something different and unique to that person. However, most men will feel ignited and aroused sexually when a woman holds him in her love, even if it's just meant for comfort, neutral and not for sexual reasons.

When a man is requesting comfort, support, and love from his woman, and asks her to hold him, most of the time this will turn into arousal for him. He doesn't mean to become aroused, it's just in his nature. Men who have done a lot of their inner work, or don't have a lot to process, especially will feel easy to rise in his erection when laying with her. Even men that do have a lot to process will still have an erection. In a lot of ways, men are like dogs with their arousal. It just peaks to arousal and springs up very quickly. However, men are certainly not dogs. They are beautiful, sensual, radiant, sexy, sexual, and dynamic beings who often have enormous hearts they just want to share with the woman they love.

When men receive the love, nurturing, support, and comfort they are craving, it often responds with his beautiful erect cock, that is just a natural part of his amazing body. A man's erect cock is an extension of his heart, and so I call it 'The Love Cock,' for so many reasons.

Usually, the men who struggle to engorge, and they are unable to become erect, is a result of what happens after being in a relationship for a while. Sometimes their heart feels shut down, closed off, they feel repressed from being their natural self, and this causes them to be unable to become erect. Some men are more guarded initially or become more guarded. Perhaps they are ready to end the relationship, or they are not quite complete or resolved from a previous relationship and their heart isn't fully open to the new person yet. If they are angry at their Beloved and haven't processed the anger, this will also cause them to remain soft. Fear also can cause them to remain soft, fear of the past, the present or the unknown future. There are many things that can close down a man's heart, however, his 'Love Cock' and erection is a direct result of his heart chakra and the energy inside his heart and his true feelings within. Once he has awareness on this, does his personal work on it, releases what he's holding onto, his 'Love Cock' can return.

The goal of hugging and holding a man is not for him to become erect or aroused, however, the knowledge of why he does not is very helpful to his healing process.

Once his 'Love Cock' returns, and he is fully in his heart, then he will be able to give love and healing to his Beloved. However, if he expects sexual gratification from his partner right away, he won't be giving his partner healing. He is still looking to receive at this point. There is a balance. There's always giving and receiving. However, both partners need to give and receive for healing to be experienced, the love energy to expand and open both partners hearts, and the sensual bliss energy to grow before full connection to take place.

Continuing to give him healing by holding him is crucial at this point, and remaining strong in yourself that nothing sexual will be happening at this time. He may beg for sex, plead, or bargain with you. It is extremely important that you stay strong in your boundaries, and only hold him right now. This is his healing session of being held. Giving him sexual gratification takes away the power of actually healing his heart. All the energy that is still in his heart will still be trapped in there if you just give in and allow him to have an orgasm and ejaculation right away. He won't grow, and he won't help you grow either. You'll just be two bunny rabbits bouncing off each other's sexual energy and the energy will blow out quickly. Once the energy bleeds out completely, he'll be drained and won't have any energy to raise his energy to expand his capacity for growth or transformation. He'll just be begging for more and more sex, or he'll just be running to the next partner looking for that bliss high and repeat the cycle. Or he'll be bored, tired and lethargic. Be the powerful Goddess that you are, and be his Healer, and make him wait and hold in his seed. Then you both reap the rewards.

Belly Massage

"Wow. I am the luckiest guy on Earth. It's no surprise that I tell you it truly opens my heart. Many nights I am laying next to Asttarte and wondering how I am going to cuddle with all the days thoughts racing through my head. So, recently I have finally begun to ask for what I need.

"Hunny, can you massage my belly?" Paavo said.

Asttarte almost always says yes. So, she slowly massages me in the belly area ever so slowly moving around my heart, lower belly and back down too right above the pubic bone. It feels like I am a baby once again slowly being rocked to sleep. I find myself melting away the days thoughts and sometimes I have tears dripping from my eyes.

It's like magic. I almost always become aroused, but it's more of a heart arousal. I start making moaning sounds of pleasure only she can hardly hear and releasing any energy that is stuck in my body.

We end up holding each other with a mutual love in which she tells me we are just building the energy hunny.

Wow…I am the luckiest guy on Earth." Paavo concluded.

A Belly Massage is the beginning of getting in touch with a man's heart. Although often men are tuned into their arousal at first and don't realize its their hearts that have been awakened. A man's vulnerability often starts with his belly, as he unravels his armor for touch, and gets closer to his needs for being loved, his heart slowly starts to melt and open. My beloved Paavo taught me about a man's heart more than any man I ever knew.

As he surrendered in those moments when I massaged him, I saw his true heart. I got to witness his authentic feelings and deep pain of wanting to be loved more than anything in the world. His longing for love was greater than anyone I ever knew. There was a huge part of him that didn't believe he was loved and didn't know how to truly love himself alone, and as I supported him in his healing process, I got to love him for the time we were together, for as long as he allowed me to love him.

When a man allows you to massage his belly, he is giving you permission to touch his heart. He is giving you permission to see inside his soul. He is giving you permission to take control of his body for those moments you touch him. And when he allows you to embrace him, he will melt into your arms like an innocent child who desperately needs to be filled with love.

Underneath the touch of a belly massage, is a deep surrender to all the layers of the emotional body, within the energy centers that his belly carries. The belly is connected to all the meridians, acupuncture points, chakras, and the hara that carries within it what the experts call the second brain. The belly is the central area of the body, and all the major organs run all throughout it. Within each organ, in Chinese medicine, is where the life force energy is stored, and how we process and run energy through our bodies. When energy is stuck, the energy cannot flow. When emotions are trapped in the organs, the body is limited with how each organ can pass energy from one organ to another. The chi energy can either flow or stop energy from flowing. When the energy stops flowing, this is when we can hold onto energy and emotions can get stuck in the body and illness can develop. When emotions remain unprocessed, deeper diseases or illnesses can develop. When emotions have a chance to be released, the chi can flow again, anger or tears can release, and health and wellness can return.

When the Goddess, Shakti, Wife or Beloved Partner massages her man (or partner), she is supporting him to release the energy and emotions that may have been inside of him for a long time. If he had been carrying energy in his belly for a lifetime and this is the first time he is releasing energy, he may need a lot more loving touch than just one session. It is important to continue to give him love many more times in this way. So, for 3 years, I gave healing sessions to my Beloved to help continue to support the release of his emotions trapped in his body.

Sometimes we need to take breaks from giving sessions to our partner, and it is important that they receive healing sessions from other people, so you do not feel drained or emptied out from giving to your partner so often.

If you feel that your partner is pulling on your energy and needs a lot of your attention, it is important to spread that energy so you can continue to support your partner in this way. Moderation is the key to everything in life, and finding a balance with giving and receiving, and making sure the rest of your life has the support it needs so you can continue to come back to each other again and again.

Enchanted Heart

Written for Asttarte

June 26, 2017

By Paavo

Hearts

Dreams

Eyes – closing

Memories

Eyes

River flows

Taking time

Wanting you

Openness

Caring

Caress

Softness

Sweet

Kisses

Hugs

Joy

Sunrise

Moonlight

Across my lips

Searching reaching

Stillness

Sunrises – eyes meet

Gazing between

The shadow

From the sunlit room

Night was full of dreams

Angels singing with joy

Marching through the clouds

Winds chimes screaming

Lots of soul searching

Eyes melting, reaching

Towards each other's

Souls are marching

Trusting caressing

Tiptoe toward her heart

Wanting her taste

Eyes gazing, touching

Brings us present

As I reach across

The meadow of our worlds,

Our fingertips touch

The tingling begins

Lunging towards her

River of weakness

One, slow, too slow

So ever slowing

Entering her

Slow, slow, lips soften

Our hearts scream for joy

The town bell rings

The angels come to us

The slow love has created joy

The child appears

The moonlight shines

Sliding deeper and deeper

The end is near

But don't you fear

We brought together

Our Enchanted Hearts.

Poem Dedicated to my Great Goddess, Teacher, Mentor, Lover and most importantly, my Beloved Asttarte!

Love, Paavo

Section 6: For Couples

The Heart On   Asttarte Deva

Understanding Intimacy

Understanding Intimacy involves Recreating Communication. Recreating Communication means repeating back to your partner what he or she said, like a mirror reflection. They then get to experience through your reflection how they feel and giving them back what they said to you so that they feel heard, understood, respected, loved, and gotten. When someone's communication is gotten, they feel whole, complete, and fully heard. And at the same time, they feel gotten they get to release the energy of what they said so that it gets to be released, and the power of intensity of it disappears.

Understanding Intimacy also includes the Importance in Sharing How You're Feeling. When you share how you're feeling, you're also sharing what's going on with your energy, you're sharing what's going on with your body, you share what's going on with your spirit, and also share what's going on with your heart and your mind.

When your share what's going on with these different elements and aspects of your being, it helps your Beloved Shakti to help you. Your energy is a part of how you're feeling. Energy gets a chance to release and lessen the pressure it is trapped in your physical body or energy body. It helps your Shakti woman feel close to you when she can help you.

It's important not to take on everything and deal with everything all by yourself. You're not taking care of you when you take on everything alone!

Say to your Beloved, "I want to be there for you honey! I can't do that when you don't let me coach you or help you or support you and you try to pull stuff out of me."

Ways to Surrender to Your Beloved And Help Her Help you:

- Admit what's going on with yourself
- Be Present
- Open the Throat Chakra
- Stop Suffering
- Be Direct – Not backwards with your Communication!

Understanding Tantric Energy Frequency Between Two Lovers

It was the middle of the night. We woke up near the morning but not early enough that we could skip the rest of our sleep for the night. It was 5 am, and I had been feeling this vibration over and over while sleeping next to my Beloved. I was in such deep sleep, but his energy had aroused me for nearly an hour. His body was moving inward and outward of his spine. Each movement forward from his side facing away from me with his face at the wall, his back side would tap my hips. He continued in this energy like he was having an orgasmic dream and moving in a dance with it that he gently bumped and tapped my hips over and over again. I awoke from my sleep so freaking aroused that I nearly jumped on top of him. I woke up and turned to face him. I put my arms around him, and my hand gently touched his belly. I put my head on his shoulder and nearly put all of my arms around him, gently moaning and kneading his stomach. I continued breathing. I was so filled with his love and energy that I nearly felt my kundalini jump out of my skin. I jumped on top of him and wanted to put him inside me right away. He was so pulled out of his comfort zone, and he had "no" idea why I was so excited and turned on. I was nearly growling, and he said, "hunny, I need you to kiss me a little bit!" I couldn't slow down. I didn't know what to do. I was perplexed and impatient. I wanted him "now" and "no" was not an option. But after my second attempt, I heard him quietly mumble, "*No, I'm not worthy!*"

Instead of ignoring his comment, I immediately reacted. I said, "*Ok, No, fine then!*" Just as I said this he was growing, and responding to my moans prior, my grabbing and demanding sex. But I had already moved to the next decision in my brain and the chemicals took over. I couldn't let it go. I said again, "*No, you said No. Forget it then!*"

He couldn't believe I reacted. He said, "*Fine then, I'll get soft!*"

I said, "*No, please don't do that!*"

But it was too late. He got soft, and he couldn't get it back.

I said, "*Hunny, you are worthy, and I want you!*"

He said, "*It's too late! I guess I'm a like a girl. I need more time to work up to you. I can't believe you're so turned on.*"

I said, "*Uh, Yes, you turned me on in your sleep that you woke me up. It was about an hour and I'm all the way excited and open.*"

He said, *"I'm sorry. I can't get it back. I'm not worthy!"*

I was mad at myself that I first said, "No, fine then." But it was too late.

I said to him, "You're so worthy." But he didn't listen.

I didn't know why I reacted. I couldn't control it. I had done all this training to help me not to react, and here I was reacting again. What was going on? I couldn't change his mind.

He already made the decision that he was unworthy and hurt for me shutting him down. But I was thrilled and excited I was open again. It felt like it had been a year since I started working on myself, after we first got together. I had been healing so many layers and levels of my childhood with him, my relationship with my mother, father and grandmother that kept me tortured throughout my adulthood. I had never been able to let someone truly in that I got close to. We had worked really hard to get here, and where I was this open and aroused to be with him. It had been a year and ½ of healing my inner child. Because I was this passionate and grateful about being open to him, I was just as mad at him shutting me down that I turned him down and my arousal disappeared.

He couldn't go back to sleep. He couldn't stay in the bed. He was irritated, dismissive and sad. He usually wants to eat in the middle of the night, even if it's just a brief moment of being awoken. It's also a sort of stress reaction that works for him to grab a snack or make something to eat. Luckily, he has a good metabolism, and he is pretty physical that he doesn't show any weight. I'm grateful for that but was actually frustrated that he was leaving and still wanted him badly. He had turned me down, because he felt "I'm not worthy and I don't matter!" But that's just a point of view. It's not true. It's just how he felt in the moment. We sort of bring these points of view about ourselves to each other, a test to see if we can let them go and grow stronger in our love for ourselves and our love for one another.

He walked away, down to the kitchen of our new home, and I couldn't sit with my energy. I completed myself so I could potentially rest and relax. He was even more upset I did this, but I couldn't get rid of the energy after it had risen so high. It was a struggle to bring it down, and I knew from the past that bringing it down only shut me down more, so I had to remove myself from my torture and hope we would make love again very soon!

If we are to grow as leaders in the community, to support, coach, and cause transformation for our clients, our friends and family, we have to be a role model and live by example. We can't be a muck and a mess and also be supporting others. It doesn't go hand in hand. There's no way to have people be able to come to us for healing, if we are arguing our points of view, or fighting with the other. If we can't heal our fears of not being loved, abandoned or worthy, there's no way we can have a healing practice for others, singles, or couples.

My goal is to have a thriving community, be a coach for couples, women and men, and be powerful enough in myself that I can remain strong, be powerful, confident and secure. My practice as a Tantra Teacher, Coach and Healer will be unsuccessful if there is no alignment, no structure, or strength between my Beloved and I.

The main goal is that we gain strength within ourselves, and as we do this, we gain strength together as a couple.

As we trust the flow of energy within ourselves, create a rhythm of love making at each appropriate and perfect time, be consistent with spiritual energy practices and support towards our goals as leaders, teachers, coaches and healers of the community, we will continue letting go of the small stuff. We will not feed into doubt, darkness or fear, and be filled with the possibility of being love, compassionate, accepting, understanding, supportive, giving, patient and kind with each other. We will have the world and the world will have us. We will be a gift to the world, a contribution on the planet, and making a difference to those who cross our paths, and our life will be filled with meaning and purpose.

As I, Asttarte, Tantrica, Dakini and Coach, will promise to continue to teach my Beloved the ways of Tantra, be accepting, loving, open, and willing, to dive deep into the depths of Shamanic Soul-searching love, Spiritual Healing, and bliss. We will have the gifts to show others why being a strong solid couple, who has knowledge, experience and wisdom; of advanced tantra, ascension teachings and meditations, powerful emotional processing and emotional clearing tools for physical and energy healing onto each other, and distinctions in ways of being, communicating, talking and acting that are in alignment with a strong solid committed loving relationship. With this, nothing can shake our ground or bring us fear of anything but profound divine union, commitment with each other, and the goal of utter bliss and ecstasy, that life is worth living and becomes heaven on earth!

His writing after this experience had a different view, a different response but yet, the same passion, the same fire and an equal amount of heart. Here are his words below. He wrote it as though he was me, in the 1st person, from his perspective.

~~~~~~~~~~~~~~~~~~~~

I Will Always Love 12/04, by Paavo, he writing as if he was Asttarte, through her eyes.

I have been in love with my man for over two years now. I mean the real thing.... heartfelt true love.

It all started two in half years ago when this hunk of a man walked into my healing session.

He discovered me the night before surfing the web in his desperate search for true love. He somehow found my True Tantra site. He ended up watching all night long each and every one of my videos and by 9am sharp he called me from his country home and with an immediate connection he got in his car and ran down to my healing studio, and we had a cup of tea and as he walked out of my office he turned around and gave me his beautiful smile and said, "sign me up". Let's give it 6 months and see if you can help me. Deep down somewhere in my subconscious I felt like he was guided by my Angels.

I spent ten long painful years hoping, wishing that the father of my child would somehow give me the love I desperately searched. In retrospect two years after many hours of Shamanic journeys, EMDR and you name it he was really my Narcissistic mother dressed up in some self-delusion that he was my everything.

Well getting back to my new client and dreaming about that crazy coincidence that only Five Days earlier I swore to myself that I would always love 12/04.

To my knowing now that it was a back-door joke that my Angels were playing on me when my new client Paavo said that his birthday was 12/04.

The following Monday, Paavo my new client walked into my healing room, and we spent hours in meditation. He was so willing to learn everything I had to offer him. Vibrational Therapy, Tantra, breath work, cord cutting, aura cleansing, eye gazing. It went on every three days he would show up at my door with an intention for our session and within seconds...literally hours he was leaving our session as though he was flying out the door.

You have to understand that I had become hard, distant and above all very professional, never even thinking about a client-lover. Well, it was an amazing seven-month ride with this human being who was saying goodbye and I don't know what got into me. I just jumped in his arms and as he walked out of our final session, I immediately went into two weeks of self-torture about "This can't be right." Against all my values as a professional how I could I feel a love for this man? My heart was finally feeling open like never before. My body trembled, and I wrote him an email telling him how mad I was that I felt so much love for him. He cried and hung up on me. I was scared I ruined everything. "Why did I tell him I was attracted to him?" OMG.

It was only two hours later where I heard this voice outside my window..." Asttarte, it's me. Let me in!" and I did. And since that day it's been the most amazing two years ever. He never left...

Months of holding each other, crying, laughing, making real heart felt love. Most importantly, Paavo began to help me heal. Wow it was real.

We spent 10 separate nights on Shamanic Journeys, hiking and dreaming.

So, I want to wrap this up, so I can share this story with all of you. Last month my Beloved Paavo rented a beautiful home for us. We are actually going to open a couple's practice. My new focus is on women, couples and men who truly want to heal.

So, for all this I say that this is actually my best Christmas Ever. Wow a real dream come true.

I Will Always Love 12/04.

Letting My Beloved Into My Heart, by Paavo

It was only a few days ago that I actually realized that in order for me to let my beloved into my heart I had to let her begin to work on me now.

My pattern in my life has been the fixer-healer for the few beloveds I have had in my 62 years.

When a person has the fixer mentality it's wonderful for a year -2 but ultimately after that person truly heals their wounds and no longer is wanting healing. Your beloved starts freaking out that what a control freak you are -dominator and eventually tells you "I can't be with you anymore". We break up and I am left blown away, feeling used and most importantly my heart shut so tight it might become impossible to ever let a healthy person back into my life. Is it worth it to be that fixer- protective mode when it actually is so destructive for both parties? It's just a distraction- protection that I patterned in my brain to protect my heart. Kind of like my heart is like an artichoke, prickly on the outside and so soft on the inside. But eventually if this pattern is continued my heart becomes prickly through and through.

It was day one when Asttarte my beloved starting a session with me. The Intention was for me to let go and let her work on me. She had me lay on my stomach and lightly feathered into my muscles and as I went into my body and placed my monkey mind on hold.

It was astounding. I was moaning like never before. At that moment, I realized that in 62 years young that no one, not even my mother had ever touched me like that. I began to scream in between full body kundalini orgasms. Wow I began to see colors and bang she was in my heart with my permission, and it was un-freaking believable. The session lasted one hour. I used to hate her working on me because I now see it was the fear of letting love inside for enough time to actually feel another human being.

Wow, to my great surprise me opening slowly that Asttarte began to feel me in her heart for her first time since we had that first six-month relationship where everyone lives in the start of a new relationship.

Wow she flipped me like a soft-boiled egg I was on my back feeling what it's like to be felt. I even felt and heard and suddenly a millionth of an inch of love energy flowing through me. My entire body was so overheated and man what a first session.

It was incredible to recognize that if we went straight to sex, it would have ruined that incredible experience that just occurred. My baby said, "I love you" and for one of the first times ever I heard her. Wow, like to energy spirits connecting on that blissful vibration of joy, peace, and love.

We laid down holding each other breathing and connecting our heart energies as we both melted into each other and fell into the depths of our deep dream like excitement. OMG I just received that living as a healer one must allow their beloved to give in the healing or the other will always feel dominated and no connection.

I will keep you posted. Wow I am even starting to taste trust. Trust is a heartfelt experience...you can't make this shit up. Asttarte my love you are it. Wow just saying these words just makes it so damn exciting.

Holding Space for Him

It's been about a week of nonstop breakdowns and breakthroughs with my beloved I only wish that we've been writing down them every single day. Writing them down every day would help to see the progress that we are making but I am sure that we are making headway into an extraordinary life that we've never dreamed possible. Each day that we have a breakdown it takes less time to get to the breakthrough. It seems as though it started with a five hour break down and then moved to three hours and then move to an hour and a half and then last night it seemed maybe about an hour or half an hour so each day the time it takes to come back to balance and back into the heart and to love it shorter and shorter.

Last night when my beloved was in a triggered state getting upset that I had a moment of anger. Then he brought up his past and an intimate experience that he had when he was a little boy, perhaps so young that he doesn't remember the duration of time or what was done. He just knew that there was a strange interaction with a family member which most all of us do as part of our growing up years.

I found myself getting upset about this interaction and I had to get up and walk away and go in another room to take a moment to breathe and relax. When I came back and let him know that I just had a moment of anger that he was so angry at the fact that I was triggered. He then went into this rage of how sexual of a person I am, how much interaction I've had, how much sexual experiences I've had, and how angry he is that I am not some virgin that's had only a couple of experiences a sexual intimacy throughout my life.

I expressed to him that this is not possible that I am an adult woman in my mid 40s now and there's no way possible that I would only have a couple interactions of intimacy. I expressed that its especially impossible given that I am a Sex Coach, Intimacy Healer and Tantrica. But especially since I've had at least a dozen times having been raped as a young woman and young teenager. The intimacy alone that I had to experience in order to help heal from these inappropriate sexual experience is well above and beyond just a couple times that he was wishing, ie a virgin.

I understand he's very conservative and old-fashioned but there is no way possible that I would be someone who had such an infinitesimal amount of experiences when he came to me as his Sex Coach and Sexual Healer.

He was in his triggered moment justifying why he was so angry at me for having so many experiences and having the ease in talking about them during any moment, with anyone and while we were making love. He was in such shock I could say things so comfortably at any time, that he requested I speak of these things to its fullest degree and acted like a lawyer pushing and pulling for me to give him any and all information of experiences that I've had, but this in fact just made him angrier. So, as he was going on about how justified he is that it's just not acceptable for him to be in love with someone who is so experienced, who has so much knowledge, who has wisdom and openness about her sexuality, that he was furious about it.

He was so upset that I would express these things freely upon questioning or upon observation, or just when I had a moment where I needed to say something, that it went so above and beyond his comfort. His frustration that he hasn't had those experiences or that he's had to listen to them made him so uncomfortable. It felt almost like a jealousy and competition to see who had more experience and who could talk about it more elaborately than the other.

The best I could do was just listen.

And, so I said, "I hear you. I get you. I understand this is extremely upsetting. I understand that you just want somebody who is a virgin, and you want somebody who has no experience and you're very angry and frustrated and you just can't deal with how it makes you feel."

I continued to re-create him and repeat what he said, and he continued to go on.

He would say "I just can't deal with this anymore. I'm moving out. I'm leaving. I'm ready to crash into the wall. I'm ready to take off and stay somewhere else."

I went into the other room, and I found a beautiful lingerie item that I hadn't worn or purchased since probably in my Early 20s, perhaps 23 and perhaps with my first husband at that young of an age. (As I had married my first husband very young.) I put this on just with a curious mind, wondering if it would still fit, wondering if I would be able to get it on, and wondering how it would feel on my body. I discovered that it did fit me and my clothes were on the floor. My outfit was on, and I stood still, perfectly fitting this sexy lingerie item from my early 20s when I was fit and petite. Suddenly, he looked up at me and said, "what was I talking about?"

Then I proceeded to tell him what he was talking about, and all of a sudden all of the anger, and the upset, and the fear and the confusion and the frustration and sadness disappeared. He didn't understand why it disappeared either. He didn't understand how all the chemicals in his brain had just gone haywire for a little while. And I continued to re-create what he said. I continued to repeat what he said, and what he was upset about and within moments he was at peace. He was relaxed.

He looked at me, eyes focused, and his mouth dropped.

He said "Oh my God. You are like a Mermaid that just came out of the ocean, and you came to this planet and entered this world with 1 million experiences and you're here with me. Why is it that I have captured the most beautiful Goddess on the planet? Why is it that she wants me? I don't understand why she would want me after having so many experiences and having been with so many men, why she would choose me."

And then all of a sudden, he realized that his feelings of not being worthy had come up, and the anger that he had was that he didn't know how to receive love. He didn't know how to take my love in, and he just wanted to shout it out because he was afraid. And so, I continued to just listen and be present and stare into his eyes. His heart melted. his eyes melted. Now all he wanted to do was just stare and breathe, and he felt this euphoric blissful feeling that was running over him. I felt it too and we just sat there breathing, looking at each other, holding presence, holding space, relaxing, and breathing. We spent the rest of the night talking about the magic of opening the heart, and the magic of healing the mind of a traumatized child and a traumatized brain. We spoke about the gift that we have in experiencing healing our minds by being together, by having one of us to be strong while the other is weak and knowing that we will come out of this as Shiva and Shakti, Shiva and Kali, Radha, and Krishna. Both powerful healer's, both able to give to the world, both able to receive the deepest love we ever wanted and never imagined possible.

Listen More Speak Less

Be Yourself
Speak less
Open your ear chakras
And let your voice be less
Slow down your thoughts
More listening

Open your sound to listening
Listen to others
Read your book on The Art of Listening
Your cat is your teacher
Practice More mantras
More regularly
Ask for help when you need it
Make requests
Share your wisdom
You are the winner
You've won the prize
You've become you
Share how you've accomplished this
You have already got there
You've won you
There is no competition
You did it
You got there
Share what you know
No pushing others to your agenda
Share your experience
You win by listening and being you
Slowing down
Get up and take actions
Go forward
And see the light
Be the light
Be the one other's look to
Show by example

Other don't have the wisdom or experience you have
Get on the calls
Follow through with your tasks
Take control
Of your own center
Rest when your mind is busy
Don't rush results
Don't rush
Slow down
Be the light others need
You are already what you need to be
Participate and join more
Let go
Be grateful
Share your gratitude
Share your love ☐
Take your own advice
You are love.

~Asttarte

Relationships as a Tool for Growth

Relationships are the most powerful tool for growth. You can do therapy for years, counseling, meditation, practices, yoga, and many other things, but the one most powerful thing that will help you to grow is intimate relationships. Someone that knows you at your core, someone that loves you at your core, or someone who has witnessed you and experienced you on a profoundly intimate level. Relationships are growth when you love someone and all the issues that have to do with love come to the surface, fear of loss, fear of abandonment, fear of rejection, fear of being controlled, fear of suffocation, air, sabotage, fear of losing one's identity, fear of losing one's individuality and independence, and all such fears that have to either do with Coming closer to the soul self, or the other.

The closer you come to the other, actually the closer you come to the self. Sometimes, going deep within, can be very scary, because we see our biggest demons there, the shadow of our self, of our inner self, our inner wounds, of our inner fears, and our greatest love.

We get to discover how deeply we love our parents when we deeply love our partner when we deeply love ourselves.

We get a chance to see all of ourselves and the other. We get a chance to see our souls. Our true selves, our innocent selves, and our radiant selves.

Only when we were afraid to see our true selves, is when issues come up with the other. When we're angry at ourselves, when we blame ourselves when we judge ourselves, when we reject ourselves is when we hurt the other.

It's only when we're afraid of being abandoned when we cling and hold tight to our partners, and we don't let them be who they are. We become possessive, jealous, controlling, and we stop our beloved, from being their true selves.

In the height of passion in a new relationship, which is often called NRE, new relationship, energy, and we don't see these things yet. They come later they come in the darkness comes. In the beginning in the honeymoon phase, our passions are aroused, we have many orgasms. We feel bliss. We adore the other. We pamper the other. We want their love. We want their approval. We want their acceptance. We want their commitment and devotion, and we'll do whatever we can to keep it even if it's to the detriment of our own freedom, free will, Joy, and our longing, and the truth of who we are.

Eventually, the truth comes out, and our real selves are revealed. We can't hide ourselves forever or pretend to be someone that we're not for very long.

So, our greatest growth happens in intimate partnerships, even really close friends. But the deepest growth happens with someone that we are in love with. It happens with someone we are making love to regularly, perhaps living together or living in close proximity to, and are deeply committed to her in whatever form that looks like, and a consistent relationship over a long period of time.

We get to discover our greatest wants, needs and desires when we're close to someone, and we don't want what they're giving. We get to discover what we don't want when we're getting something that deters us, or we're not interested in.

We get to discover what we really want when we get a taste of it, but only a small piece of it and we want more of it.

There are so many layers of ourselves to discover to unravel, and to transform. We can spend our entire lives, transforming ourselves to become greater people and humans on the planet with a partner by your side. It helps to go deeper within, discover the truth of who you are discover your greatest strength, greatest power, and your greatest weaknesses. Without another, to reflect on, to reflect back to you, we often stay in the dark, and in the unknown. We often only grow so much. We often may stay small, or we can hide in the other relying on them to give us our strength, our power, and our will, but without these experiences, we don't know. So, experience love, experience growth, experience transformation, and experience your true self. Love with your whole heart, and with your truth.

Writing Exercise: Questions For Couples

Do two soul mates who want to build a life of heart and happiness need to constantly go to healing events (therapy, maintain a spiritual practice, etc) to stay open and alter their soul so they can continue to love one another throughout their relationship?

How does a couple know if their arousal is coming from the heart or coming from need?

Do both partners need to be trigger-less before true heart on can be connected during an ascension meditation?

No, the heart rises its energy while the triggers lessen during meditation and the chemicals in the brain get less as the euphoria of meditation rises.

When you wake up after a romantic dream with your Beloved that's been in your arms all night, can you even really connect with her if her yoni is in a solid freeze?

Does your Beloved in that freeze feel guilty in honoring your hardness or shut down her heart more?

Contemplate on these questions, and try answering them in your notebook to the best of your ability. There is no right answer. The only right answer is what's right for you.

The Heart On   Asttarte Deva

Wild Tantric Review, by Paavo

Today is January 2 and I just went up to bed with my Beloved Asttarte and had one of the biggest revelations in my entire life for myself. As I was laying next to her, she had me put my hand on her Yoni. I was really in my head because I'm doing a lot of work now for the business and usually when I'm in my thinking head it's hard for me to connect to my heart. So, what I did was, I put my hand on her Yoni, and she cried. Then I actually had a revelation, that her crying was her healing her heart.

I saw that so internally; I also saw in this session that I have always been in a performance mode. I am not giving my heart the opportunity to be present in stillness and slowness and connection to my Beloved's heart; only once in a while am I going to do it right.

Like wow, oh my heart, and I'm thinking, "how hard I am. Am I going to be big enough? Am I giving her the right penetration? Am I saying the right words, did I touch the wrong place?"

So, what we began to do was some reading, and we were activating our Kundalini's a little bit. As soon as we were about to make love, and I always wait for Asttarte to make the go ahead. Right, because I'm someone that's courteous that wants everybody to be happy. I'm that kind of guy.

So, she says before I say anything. "I wonder what position we should do!" blah blah blah blah blah, so it took me from my heart to my head, not the head of my cock, but the head of the brain.

Then I got soft immediately, and then what happened afterwards, Asttarte actually said, "Everything's OK Honey. Let me hold you. Let's just go back to feeling each other."

And, at that moment I realized just like that, my whole life I have been mourning that I never did want to hear her, that I did something wrong, because really in the end, I've been a beaten dog all my life. I was so beaten, and I got it that I thought people don't love me. So, my point of view is, I guess, that "I need to perform, and be perfect, and you can beat me." Oh, my that's one hell of a way to live! So, in the end, my Beloved grabbed me and told me it was OK, and as I found my body getting looser and looser, and my head was on her heart, I felt a connection like never before.

I actually bawled my eyes out for about five minutes, and the feeling that I had, to healing, was recognizing the pain that I have been in my whole life of always being in the point of view, is that "I'm not worthy of talking. I'm not worthy and I talk too much, and I am not OK."

And then what happened, at that moment, after I cried and I connected my behavior my whole life of wanting to fix my lover, "which I have been doing a great job at healing her", but anytime something goes wrong I become the beaten dog. I don't really hear her. For me, I'm always working on "Who is working me?"

Towards my Beloved, whoever that is at the time, I'm in fixing mode. I'm in a performance mode. I'm in the beaten dog mode. And then today the revelation was there! Once I cried, I could see that all at once! And I took a deep breath. I breathed in a lot. I said, "I finally feel your love."

And she said, "No you finally let me in."

From that experience, I totally connected that I don't let her in, because I'm feeling like a beaten dog, and I'm always fixing somebody.

Then ultimately the crazy ones that I got involved with in my whole life; the six or seven so called loves of my life, were all crazy. And my job was to fix them. In the end when they got healthy, they got tired of me. If you're a beaten dog your whole life, you don't see that the person in front of you loves you so much.

What I saw today is that Asttarte loves me so much, that she sees all the powerful tools that we have for and with each other, for ourselves and how amazing of a life we can have. But I'm never really here, *because I'm involved in being perfect with this other bullshit with the business and the lawyers and the bankruptcy and reality. And the only way that's going to work is if I create a future, you know a game in the world, for each little thing that I have that's important.*

And the big thing with the garden and the kids that's all happening too, but really in the end, I realized it like it's maybe not as much as my sexual insecurity with Asttarte. It's just 100% been my trust for anybody, and I just saw that it's me that's been holding myself back, by not asking for what I need. Getting what I need and having a person as compassionate and loving and empathic and powerful as Asttarte, is to actually help me heal. Holy shit. What a revelation!"

One last note, I have to tell you, that before we were holding each other, I realized that after Asttarte had opened her heart. So, what are you doing after Asttarte opened her heart so deeply the other night and wanted me to take a bath. I didn't understand that she wanted me to ground her, so when she came back in the bed, the tip of her yoni was closed because she felt shut down. Then I got triggered because I live with a woman that's all she did was practice self-love, so how cool is that!

I finally realize like if I just stay present, shut my mouth, be more in touch with her, feel my feelings, ask her what I need, open my heart, and cry, I might never be insecure, not ever. But like it's a beginning for me to at least experience that I bring it on myself. It's not them doing anything. It's really all about me and my lack of self-awareness. And that's OK. I'm OK with it. Well, I actually just said I'm OK with not being perfect. OK that's it for now.

The Heart On   Asttarte Deva

Section 7: Tantric & Relationship Exercises for Keeping the Heart Open

The Heart On   Asttarte Deva

Some Tantra practices you can start with are:

Creating a Sacred Bubble (Laurie Handlers style).
Face each other. The masculine partner on the bottom, while the feminine's legs overlay her/she's partners legs. Sit far enough from each other that you can still look into each other's eyes, but legs are overlapping each other's a little bit. Breathe in, lift your arms above and over your own head, up to the sky, and down your back, then to your own heart. Then, lift your arms up and over your partners head and down their back, almost touching their lower back. Then lift your arms up again, and over your partners head and towards your own heart, stopping at your heart center. You both have your hands in prayer position, where the hands touch each other. Then breath in and bring your foreheads together ending with the sacred kiss. Here you can state your intention with your tantric practice together, and any boundaries you currently have, or issues you might be dealing with. You can also state your pleasure here.

Eye Gazing for at least 5 minutes with each other. The eye gazing practice releases the armor around the eyes so when there are moments of gazing into each other's eyes, you are able to be more vulnerable with each other, melt into each other's eyes, cry if you are touched, moved, or inspired, and your heart feels open or starts to open. Eye Gazing builds an energy of trust, safety, and love, and there is nothing quite like it, especially being with the person you care for the most. It actually can be very powerful and magical and when performed for a length of time, the energy just melts deeper and deeper and can be quite blissful.

Meditation facing each Other. Meditation while facing each other in the lotus position over time allows the energy of the chakras to melt, clear, expand and connect to each other. Meditating facing another person is a very intimate practice and if you don't want to melt the armor with another person or want to keep your distance, do a different practice. If you do want to feel close and build a connection with someone, facing across from each other is an excellent way to build the love energy between the two of you. The best way to perform this is with knees touching, or very close to this.

Meditating Next to Your Partner. You might not think that meditating sitting next to someone builds any energy of closeness, but in fact, it truly does. It doesn't happen as quickly as the other practices above, however, it does happen. It's a rather nice feeling of neutrality, equality, and love. If you want to diminish any feelings of competition, and feel like your partners best friend, sitting next to each other will build a nice energy of love, peace, and bliss. Eventually you might want to lay your leg over the other to feel even closer. That's when you know the practice is bringing the two of you together.

Tantra Breathing – A Breathwork Meditation Facing Each Other.
One practice I love to do with my partner(s) is to do a Tantra Breathing practice while sitting across from each other. Now, in a short period of time, this will raise the kundalini energy and bring a partner to orgasmic breathing and can easily bring someone to orgasm with their clothes on. It's an excellent precursor to the real sexual act and helps to build the kundalini energy if it's not there, or to raise it even higher so that when you do physically touch on the skin, you don't have to do any sort of pumping to have an orgasmic experience. It can actually be done energetically, at least much more easily. What you do, is a circular breathing with your partner. While your partner breathes in, you breathe out. While they breathe in, they pull the energy down to the belly, then to the genital muscles, then squeeze the muscles, like a contraction, for about 4 to 6 seconds, and then exhale the breath while visualizing the energy going down the legs with the exhale. The partner breathes in through the nose, into the belly, then squeezes, while the other partner exhales the energy down the legs. That's the short version.

Picture yourself in that sacred bubble you created above. Do the practice as described above. Then visualize the energy flowing over your own body, into your own body, as you breathe, and as you exhale, see it going up from your feet, into your partners head with your exhale as they breathe in at the same time. You each see, and visualize the energy as it moves, flows, and breathes and you breathe together as though you are in synch and one. As the energy builds, the squeezing at first might be harder, but eventually the squeezing becomes pleasurable, and when the exhale comes, sometimes too does the orgasm. Feel free to do this for 10 minutes, 20 minutes, 30 minutes, or even longer as the energy continues to build. You may choose not to do anything else because this feels so amazing!

Spooning the Tantric Way. Spooning is a classical term most couples mention they would love to do, and often the fall asleep while doing this. However, once you feel the energy of love from your partner, then switch. Whoever was in front for the first 10 or so minutes, go to the back of your partner and hold them. This will create equality, and the energy will be balanced, and in fact it can build the energy between the two people. When one person is always giving, or one person is always receiving energy gets diluted, and disappears. The passion goes away when it's not shared equally. When both people in the partnership feel equally loved, received in support, and give of their love, leadership, and power, then the bliss can remain, and love stays strong.

After any, some, or all of these practices, you can choose however you want to connect next. The choice is yours. There are no limits to how you can raise the energy of your love, and in particular, your love cock, metaphorically or for real. (Yes, women with women, can use their energetic love cocks too. That's another topic for another book).

Kundalini Orgasmic Meditation

Intention: A gentle meditation practice incorporating breathing into the belly and expanding the breath throughout the entire body. Orgasmic Meditation helps to ignite pleasure in the body, feel peace, but also bliss. It is a guided meditation to channel sexual energy throughout the body, clear energy, and raise sexual and spiritual energy.

Grounding and Shielding: You will find yourself a seat in the room, choosing to sit upright or laying down on a pillow or blanket. You will start with breathing into the belly, breathing in the nose and out the mouth. Feel your connection to the earth, but also your body and the energy around you. Notice the frequency in your energy field. Get present to how you feel, and breathe that knowing into your belly, exhaling out the mouth to release any stress you feel.

Balancing: As you feel deeper into your body and feel more comfortable with your breathing, you will start to inhale in through the top of the head and exhale the breath down the legs.

Intention and Declaration: This practice is a connection to your deeper self. Whatever intention you have is for your personal awareness. Examples are: love myself deeper, love my partner deeper, clear myself of stress, remove stagnation or armor, open my heart more for giving and receiving love, gain the ability to make love longer, etc.

Completion and Grounding: As you go deeper into your breathing process, you will forget you are sitting in a room with other people, you will enjoy the pleasure of your breath, and appreciate your body more. You may have a mini full body energetic orgasm, or a HUGE one! However, you will gain a taste of the possibilities this provides, and if your energy is open, receive incredible joy from the process. As we come to a close you will breathe slower, longer, and more gently, exhaling into the earth to connect, get settled, and ground.

This is not a chakra meditation practice, but a kundalini meditation to help bring opening throughout the chakra channel, removing blocks along the central pathway of the body, and inhaling to increase the sexual energy flow, and exhaling by bringing the sexual energy down to ground.

It helps to bring awareness to how open your energy is, and also is a practice that can be learned to do on your own. It helps with erectile dysfunction, healing the prostate, elongating your love making experience and strengthening your sexual muscles for health, pleasure, and multiple orgasms. Great for men and women!

Intimacy and Touch

In this short Intimacy and Touch segment, Asttarte will lead you through a few simple intimacy practices great for couples to do together to increase their bond, trust, safety, and intimacy with one another. This practice can also be done with a stranger to help with opening your heart, learning to accept people for who they are, to see their greatness, and building the ability to let down your guard, gaining love for yourself, the ability to receive love, but also give. It helps to create a balance of giving and receiving in yourself and find the beauty and love in everything you see. The practice helps increase your appreciation for your loved one, but also life in general. To appreciate life, is to feel grateful, and with gratitude all your desires can be manifest. The practice also helps one to be seen, witnessed, and often when we are witnessed in our true authentic nature, we can more easily be our true self with others, those we love, but also strangers and life itself. To be authentic is to be the real you, and nothing creates joy more than by being who you are.

In this practice of Intimacy and Touch, couples that came together will have an opportunity to get closer and learn a couple simple practices you can take home with you. You can also partner with someone new and learn how to be vulnerable with a new person and feel safe knowing, it is new for them too.

Some practices during the 15-minute segment will be:
Belly Breathing while Eye Gazing, 5 minutes or longer as time permits for eye gazing, starting with the belly breath to get grounded and connected with your partner.
Scanning their body with your hands, non-Touch, find out where your partner felt the energy and where they did not
Firm holding pressure as your partner allows, slowly going into the position and slowly coming out.
Heart to Heart Link Connection
Holding hands to ground and close

Relationship Vision

One way you can redirect the energy of your relationship is to create a relationship vision together of your ideal life together. Sit together and discuss what your ideal relationship would be like. First you want to do a meditation to clear your energy, and picture yourself in the most ideal relationship you could ever imagine possible.

Here is an example of my partners and my Relationship Vision. Come up with your own Relationship Vision, and watch magic happen.

ASTTARTE DEVA & PAAVO

We are each other's best friends.
We cuddle each other regularly
We massage each other regularly
We love each other madly
We go to bed with love in our hearts
We have fun together, and create sensual, loving, and magical sex.
We do magick and ritual together
We express to each other when we want to make love
We cook and garden together
We watch the different Solstices together
We work together and write books together and on our own
We travel together
We go to family functions together
We give each other freedom and space when we need to
We show my son what a healthy relationship looks like
We organize Shamanic Journeys together
We trust each other and meet each other's needs
We both are in training to be Shamanic Facilitators & Leaders together
We Meditate every day, and do Magick, Energy Work, Mantras or Shamanic practices
We each have friends together and on our own.
We support each other to have many friends.

We devote time to each other every week
We are committed to each other
We are super attracted to each other
We are physically healthy, emotionally balanced, mentally sound, and financially secure
We settle our differences peacefully
We share a Spiritual practice together
We have a strong Spiritual practice on our own
We devote time each week to do Imago Therapy Sessions together, our Step Recovery work together and on our own and continue to grow stronger and become more powerful.
We devote time each week to honor each other
We accomplish big goals together
We kiss each other regularly
We support each other's goals and dreams
We encourage each other to be the best we can be
We acknowledge each other regularly
We take responsibility for our own feelings, behaviors, and actions
We restore integrity regularly
We encourage each other to be independent and to do fun things together
We are successful independently and as a couple.

Asttarte & Paavo

Gratitude Checklist

Here you can practice listing the things you are grateful for in your partner. When you emphasize the things, you are grateful for, more positive things start to happen and your relationship blossoms.

List 5 Things I am Grateful for, my life together with my Beloved.

I am grateful for her/his commitment to our relationship, wanting to work through things that bothers us about one another.

I am grateful when we cuddle, and she opens her heart to me.

I am grateful that you are always working on yourself.

I am grateful that you are a Tantra Goddess/Intuitive.

I am grateful that you know how to smile and look into my eyes and touch my soul.

I am grateful every time you are present with me.

I am grateful you hold me when I need you to.

You can come up with your own gratitude checklist. You know what you are grateful for. Come up with a list you can come back to whenever you forget and get into your head. Use your gratitude list to come back to your heart!

Start The Day Ritual

- Meditate for at least 10 minutes (before going downstairs/greeting each other

- Greet each other with a Namaste ☐

- Bow to one another

- Mouth Closed

- Don't speak until kind words come through

- "I love you!"

- Greet each other with kindness

- If feelings come up - journal them 1st

- Write each other a love note on a post it note. (Get post it notes to leave outside the doors (place in a box or mini wall shelf to hang and leave for future notes)

- If we are passionate about doing something/accomplishing something - make note of the task before walking away, then say "I love you" or "And so it is!"

- Start the Day with Tea ~ watering our plants/watering each other: shower/bath/hug

- Make a list of the tasks that need to be done

- No Coaching each other until we Coach ourselves and love ourselves first, then love each other.

- Make each other breakfast/ Think of the other

- We are One!

Phrases to Hang on the walls

I love _____, even when he/she makes me angry.

My Beloved and I always communicate when we need to.

I am patient with my Beloved and know that we all have our own way of processing and understanding things.

I know how to ask for what I need from my partner.

My partner listens to me when it is the right time for him/her.

I am loved in every moment even in moments, I don't feel like I am.

We don't have to agree on everything.

We don't have to like all the same things.

I adore _____ and _____ adores me.

I always want to make love when my heart is full.

If something is bothering me, I will be the one to initiate discussions about it.

My partner and I always love each other, and we can always work through anything.

If I can't love my partner right now, there's something in me I need to love.

If I'm upset about something and I don't know what it is, try to be patient with yourself and your partner.

I can always get my needs met if I am direct and ask for what I want.

I have a healthy, loving and fulfilling relationship.

All my sexual needs are met all the time.

I am beautiful, sexy, and loving.

I am beautiful, sexy, and lovable.

My partner is everything that I need and want.

If my partner is not fulfilling my needs, I will not withhold this information from him/her and be brave and tell the truth.

My partner and I always have fun together, and we can make up fun as we go along.

Have fun with this. Write them on post it notes around the house or create your own little cards or labels. You can make up your own too! Make it fun. You might surprise your partner and yourself.

The Heart On   Asttarte Deva

*Live this moment as totally as possible,
and suddenly you will come to realize,
that if you live it totally, it is solved.
There is no need to solve it.
Life is not a problem to be solved,
but a mystery to be lived.*

OSHO

The Heart On   Asttarte Deva

Appendix: The Brain is the block to Your…

Heart

Soul

Feelings

Presence

The brain protects the person.

It keeps the ego alive and well.

It keeps us living in the past.

It keeps the same pattern in our behaviors, repeating themselves over and over, expecting different results.

The brain keeps us in denial of any destructive behavior.

It keeps us from having intimate and loving relationships.

The heart is the key to Love

Loving ourselves

Non-judgment

Having loving and intimate relationships.

Recommended Books:

The Wisdom of Listening, by: Mark Brady

The Mastery of Love, Wisdom Book, By Don Miguel Ruiz

Blue Truth, A spiritual guide to life & death and love & sex, by: David Deida

Tantra, The Art of Conscious Loving, by: Charles and Caroline Muir

Desire. The Tantric Path to Awakening, by: Daniel Odier

Sex & Happiness; The Tantric Laws of Intimacy, by: Laurie Handlers

Embracing the Beloved, Relationship as a Path of Awakening, by: Stephen and Ondrea Levine

Intimacy; Trusting Oneself and the Other, insights for a new way of living, by: Osho

Reclaiming Eros, Sacred Whores & Healers, by: Suzanne Blackburn and Margaret Wade

Beyond Tantra, Healing through Taoist Sacred Sex, by: Micke & Stephen Wik

Reclaiming Aphrodite; The Journey to Sexual Wholeness, by: Amrita Grace

The power of Shakti, 18 Pathways to Ignite the Energy of the Divine Woman, by: Padma Aon Prakasha

Womb Wisdom, Awakening the Creative and Forgotten Powers of the Feminine, by: Padma and Anaiya Aon Prakasha

Getting the Sex You Want, Shed Your Inhibitions and Reach New Heights of Passion Together, by: Tammy Nelson, LPC

Sex and the Perfect Lover, Tao, Tantra, and the Kama Sutra, by: Mabel Iam

The Journey to Sexual Wholeness, The Six Gateways to Sacred Sexuality, by: Kypris Aster Drake

Sex Secrets of Escorts, Tips from a Pro, by: Veronica Monet

Essential Reiki, by Diane Stein

The Heart On   Asttarte Deva

Dedications

Music Dedications

Song Paavo dedicated to Asttarte:

I Want You To Have it All, Artist: Jason Mraz

Asttarte's song Dedicated to Paavo:

Hunny I'm Good, Artist Andy Grammer

Some of Paavo's Favorite Movies

Into the Wild
Waterboy
Forest Gump
Jack Ryan
No Time to Die
Spectre
50 Shades Freed
My 5 Wives
Jolt
It's a Wonderful Life
Pacific Rim
Ladybugs
Die Hard
Back to School
IQ
Serious Moonlight
The Philadelphia Story
Curb Your Enthusiasm
Iron Fist
Rainman
The Graduate

Book by Asttarte Coming Soon:

Grieving the Shamans Way; What I Learned from The Love of My Life Dying

Grieving the Shamans Way, Book Excerpt

CHANNELING SEXUAL ENERGY AND BRINGING IT TO THE HEART

When your sexual energy is so high how do you bring it to the heart? It's important to bring the energy up to the heart when you're feeling so much energy in your body and you know that it needs to come from a place of love. It's time to bring that love energy and raise it up to your heart. Your own energy is your teacher. It is your guide. It is a message to go inward. We can have energy that's really strong but when it's so strong it's looking outside, it's time to bring it inward and see it as a teacher.

How do you bring your energy up to your heart? First, it's about noticing and then after you notice it go within. Take that energy and pull it up to your heart and center yourself.

How do you pull the energy up to your heart? The first step is to notice that your sexual energy is extremely high.

If your sexual energy is mixed with high emotions that are difficult to deal with, the important thing to do is notice those emotions. If you have anger, it is imperative to process the anger. If you have grief, it is crucial to process the grief. If you feel resentment, disappointment, confusion, animosity, or any emotion where you would be projecting unloving feelings, thoughts, or behaviors onto another, the first thing to do is to become balanced within the self-first. You don't want to be putting those feelings onto other people, and especially someone you care about, or have an interest in getting close to. I talk about how you can process anger and other emotions throughout this book.

For now, we're going to go over how you can channel your sexual energy up to your heart. Once, you feel clear of any unhealthy or dark emotions, then you can channel the positive energies and emotions up to your heart.

Practice on Channeling Sexual Energy and Bringing it to Your Heart

Step 1: Start with your Breath
Do deep belly breathing, where you inhale in your nose, and exhale out your mouth. When you inhale in your nose, pull the breath fully into your belly. Let your belly expand fully as though it is sticking out from eating a full meal, or the analogy I like to use, "Like Santa Clause." Start with a count of 4 or 5, and then tilt your pelvis forward about 1 to 2 inches while squeezing your kegel muscles at the same time. The goal is to eventually squeeze the genital muscles from your anus to your inner reproductive system (where you would hold your pee if you had to urinate). After you squeeze these muscles, again, you want to hold for a count of 4 to 6, and then as you exhale, instead of exhaling the breath down the legs to raise your sexual energy or ground your energy, you want to visualize the breath going up to your heart center. As the breath is going up, your pelvis returns to normal position. Bring the breath directly to the center of your heart chakra at your breastbone area. As the energy comes to this region you should be fully at the end of your exhale.

Step 2: Continue Breathing in this Way

Continued in Book…

The Heart On   Asttarte Deva

About the Author

Asttarte Deva, born as Jennifer Rose, has been a writer her whole life, an Intuitive since birth and a Relationship, Intimacy, Love & Tantra Coach since 2005. Along the path of helping others have pleasure, intimacy, and bliss, she discovered that she too deserved true love and happiness. Upon meeting the man she describes in this book, she found her happiness, and discovered along the way that their combined efforts and experience in the Holistic Healing Arts, Yoga and Recovery they could collaborate their visions to help other couples seeking love, intimacy and profound pleasure.

Asttarte has been a practitioner in the Healing Arts most of her life, and as an adult became Certified and Trained in multiple styles of Reiki, Massage, Yoga, Tantra, Life & Transformational Coaching, Breathwork, Relationship Coaching, Sex & Intimacy and has an innate intuitive wisdom she has carried with her entire life. In her more current years, she has trained under the knowledge and guidance of multiple types of Shamans and Spirit Medicine Facilitators and now combines this wisdom with her previous work in the Healing Arts. She has also been a Writer most of her life, and she hopes you will use these volumes as guides on your journey. May they serve you, bring you knowledge and wisdom and help you on the path of your own discovery and enlightenment.

Asttarte is also the Author of Awaken to Living, Tantra for Your Whole Life, and Coming Soon: Grieving the Shamans Way, What I Learned from the Love of My Life Dying, On Bufo 5-MEO DMT, Spirit Medicine, Intimacy & Being Our Authentic Selves.

www.ingramcontent.com/pod-product-compliance
Lightning Source LLC
Chambersburg PA
CBHW071659170426
43195CB00039B/2344